I0486937

Everyone Innovates Here

Accelerating Innovation
and Entrepreneurship
Across Your Entire
Community

Della Rucker AICP CEcD
Author of The Local Economy Revolution

Also by Della Rucker

The Local Economy Revolution: What's Changed and How You Can Help.

Crowdsourcing Wisdom: a guide to doing public meetings that actually make your community better (and won't make people wish they hadn't come)

Why this Work Matters: Wisdom From the People who are Making Communities Better (ed.)

Everybody Innovates Here

Developing a higher-impact,
sustainable, inclusive and more
effective way to accelerate innovation
and entrepreneurship across your
entire economy

Wise Fool Press,
An imprint of the
Wise Economy Workshop

Copyright © 2018 Della G. Rucker. All rights reserved.

No part of this book may be transmitted or reproduced in any form by any means without permission in writing from the publisher. If you want that permission, you can contact the publisher through the web site below.

Published by Wise Fool Press, an imprint of the Wise Economy Workshop, LLC.

3570 Sherbrooke Dr.
Cincinnati, OH 45241 USA

wiseeconomy.com

For speaking, writing or other engagements, contact della.rucker@wiseeconomy.com

Produced and printed in the United States of America

ISBN for digital version: 978-0-9900044-7-9

ISBN for print version: 978-0-0-9900044-8-6

Library of Congress Control Number 20139510556

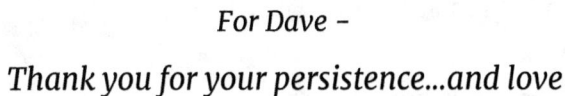

For Dave –

Thank you for your persistence...and love

Table of Contents

Part 1: An Innovation Infrastructure

Introduction

In 2013, I wrote a book called *The Local Economy Revolution* that described how conventional economic development and urban planning methods were failing to create the kind of communities we need in the emerging economic and social era. In 2015, I wrote a book called *Crowdsourcing Wisdom* that addressed one of the core failings I had identified: a systematic failure to meaningfully involve everyone in a community in making decisions about their communities' futures.

In 2016, I put two more partially- completed books on hold to work on a start up. My distraction didn't come from an app or a shop:

It came from the opportunity to build groundbreaking new systems that could enable the change I'd been grasping for.

Over the past 2 years, I've seen close-up what *systems for accelerated innovation* can do. I've watched people who haven't yet finished college equip a business to raise millions in investment. I've seen 60-year-old founders' eyes open wide when they're shown a solution they had never considered - by a team whose average age is 24. I've watched an overlooked neighborhood discover its hidden assets and find its authentic voice.

And we've partnered with innovators across the spectrum, across silos and across countries to learn more about new ways of working and doing, better and faster.

What we have learned at Econogy is:

- We need **much more innovation**, from the grassroots to the corporate, and from the social to the technical. And we need that innovation to get out of the local test, the pilot stage, much faster and more completely than its often does.

- We need, as a culture, to **get much better at innovation** if we want to have half a chance of meeting the stunning array of challenges in front of us.

- We have been **leaving innovation too much to chance**, given that it's something that we need so much. We've relied on magical thinking, unquestioned rules of thumb and feel-good anecdotes, and we've gotten haphazard results, at best -- haphazard results that waste much of our best assets.

This book captures what innovation districts, startup ecosystems and other parts of this emerging sector need to do differently if we are all to build the world that we need in the emerging era. We need:

- more innovators,

- more completely and fully diverse innovators,

- more intentional innovation growth,

- more intentional interlacing between corporate, institution, starters and non-profits, and

- more intentional effort to not only start more, but enable every start to reach its full capacity, locally or globally.

This book is part of building on what we've all done to date to get to the future we need. We hope you will join us. This is a fast-evolving subject, and no one, including me, knows what everyone is learning everywhere.

And as we are putting what we've learned into action, we know that we will find new ideas as well. To stay in touch with what everyone is learning, join us at everybodyinnovateshere.com for updates, new information and thoughtful discussion.

We're glad you're along for the journey.

How we got here

For my co-founder, Owen Raisch, and I, the purpose of Econogy has been to accelerate innovation for the places and people we care most about. That includes universities and neighborhoods, businesses and nonprofits, wealthy and disadvantaged, students and seniors. We focused our first two years on building a new machinery of innovation: a system for unlocking the capabilities and lack of barriers that one of the overlooked source of innovation - young adults - could bring to problem-solving.

We found that a **support structure that combined diverse teams, clear processes, and high-stakes stretch challenges resulted in practical but innovative solutions** to problems that had no cookie-cutter answers. From both a business and a human development standpoint, the results were better than we (well, I, at least) anticipated.

We then tried the same methods with adults of varying ages faced with creating strategy for their community's future, and we had similar results.

Consistently, people outperform our expectations when we place around them a structure that enables them to solve problems collaboratively and constructively. And innovation research has found the same:

- **Diverse teams consistently make better decisions,**[1] potentially because they "alter the behavior of a group's social majority in ways that lead to improved and more accurate group thinking."[2]

- When **teams use explicit structured processes to evaluate choices and make decisions, they are more likely to succeed.** Conversely, when leaders assume that the team will just figure it out for themselves - what I've called elsewhere "playing by the rules we learned in kindergarten" - then the team is more likely to fail.[3]

- Creating useful solutions to problems that do not have direct precedents require a fundamentally different approach than simply tweaking things that have been done before. And **being too familiar with the things that have been done before can be like a pair of blinders,** making it impossible to see feasible alternatives that fall outside your expectations.[4]

At Econogy, these experiences gave us proof of concept on something bigger: we had a small but accumulating

[1]
https://www.hcamag.com/hr-news/do-diverse-teams-perform-better-245514.aspx
[2] https://hbr.org/2016/11/why-diverse-teams-are-smarter
[3] https://hbr.org/2010/06/the-decision-driven-organization
[4]https://www.forbes.com/sites/stevedenning/2012/11/12/why-the-paradigm-shift-in-management-is-so-difficult/#4dc88c935f9

body of evidence about how we could enable people to accelerate innovation.

For someone who had spent over 20 years trying to improve problem-solving in communities as a downtown revitalization, urban planning and economic development specialist, this was the kind of insight I'd been looking for. You see, I'd become trapped by my own, conventional understanding of how economies and teams work, too.

Before co-founding Econogy, I had written a lot of lines in a lot of blogs and articles and books about how local economies needed to change, and how the ways we were pushing that to happen weren't working. I had spent hundreds of hours with tech startups, mom and pop shops, universities, microentrepreneurs, and the organizations that try to take care of them. And I knew we needed something different.

But I didn't know what.

After two years of working out the mechanisms for supporting diverse team innovation, and combining that with decades of experience with economic and community support organizations, I've come to the conclusion that **most cities need empowered innovation districts to accelerate innovation across the complete economic and community spectrum.**

There's a lot of different kinds of organizations in this process, and they go by different names in different places. So for sake of simplicity, we're going to call all of these organizations part of the Innovation Infrastructure.

An Innovation Infrastructure, as we are describing it, is a program, a place or a group of programs and places that play a role in generating more economic activity from the people who are in a community. These might include anything from a tech accelerator to a rural organic agriculture collaborative, from a university advanced manufacturing initiative to corporate new initiatives group to a peer coaching program for African-American urban residents who want to start businesses.

That's a radical statement, in case you didn't notice. Historically, we have carefully parsed these segments apart -- tech programs over here, Main Street business owners over here, rural here, urban there, bigger businesses often off by themselves. We differentiate them based on how much money they might make, where their clients live, where they will have their shop, whether we designate them as having a "social impact," and more. And yes, they will have certain needs that are specific to their unique situation.

But what we find over and over is this: **Innovators are often more similar than different.** They all need help innovating. They all need help getting out of their own paradigm. And **they can all learn from each other.**

(And yes, innovation and entrepreneurship are not exactly the same thing. We're more interested in this book in innovation on the whole, but systems designed to foster entrepreneurship are a large part of the existing infrastructure supporting potential innovators of all types. More on that in an upcoming chapter.)

Innovation Infrastructure

Want to drive yourself to drink? Try to come up with a clear, new name for something that is frequently misunderstood and not well defined...

People who work in innovation and entrepreneurship are accustomed to hearing and using all sorts of terms - and like a lot of terms, sometimes different people don't mean exactly the same thing when they use the same set of syllables. "Districts" and "Ecosystems," for example, have come into vogue lately to describe a collection of activities and programs and people working to increase or strengthen entrepreneurship in a given area, but it's not always clear what's inside or outside the ecosystem, or how exactly they do (or should) interact.

We can stretch the analogy a bit by saying that, while we might know a decent amount about the biology of individual businesses, and we might have figured out some best practices for operating some of these components, we are just at the beginning of the environmental sciences phase of understanding innovation.

Later in this book, we'll try to land on more precise definitions of these systems and their parts - as your sixth grade science teacher said, classification is crucial to being able to study something. But in the title of this chapter, I introduced a whole 'nother word -- "infrastructure."

As if this wasn't already confusing. Let me explain why.

By this point, I think most people have at least a passing familiarity with the term "infrastructure" (that wasn't the case when I started my urban planning career a couple decades ago). We've all seen enough news articles proclaiming the dire conditions of our roads, sewers, water plants, etc. to know that **infrastructure generally refers to the things and systems that most of us don't think about often, but that allow modern life to happen.** Bridges, pumping stations, canal locks, fiber optic cables, electrical transformers, rail lines...all these things make up our infrastructure.

When they fit together correctly, and each part does its job right, then they do the things we need them to do so well that we easily forget that they're there. When they don't...in the case of of physical infrastructure, we know it needs to get fixed, fast, because our civilization depends on it.

The only difference with innovation infrastructure is that it's not fully developed, and we haven't become accustomed to having it work well yet. But as we'll see in an upcoming chapter, we have to get it fully built and working, fast.

The reason why I used the term "infrastructure" instead of "ecosystems" or systems or something like that is to keep this idea in front of us: we need to **increase the *intentionality* of our work to accelerate innovation and entrepreneurship.**

When engineers prepare to build a neighborhood, or even a collection of a few buildings, they put hours upon hours into calculating electric loads, managing projected stormwater runoff, evaluating the tensile strength of the steel deck on the bridge. And they pay very close attention to **how the pieces *connect* with each other**. If the bridge deck isn't connected to the piers properly, or the substation is under-capacity for peak electric demand, or if the parking lot will triple the amount of water that rushes into the creek with a normal rain, then even the best-designed individual component will not have much benefit, and could cause a lot of damage.

It is in the *connectivity*, the interrelations, that an infrastructure does its work.

We are at a very early stage in building our innovation infrastructure. Sometimes we find that we have built a culvert that runs cross-ways to where the water is running, or we designed a road for a lot more traffic than it ended up carrying. And that's not surprising. We're still learning how to do this.

But as we will discuss, the pressures that the emerging economic era are placing on our communities and our economies and our people and businesses means that we have to **accelerate our own learning about how to build this infrastructure.** We have to get much better at it, much faster. And as early civil engineers found, sometimes that means that we have to be prepared to take apart one of the things we built, and rebuild it to tie more effectively into the system.

Let's be clear: when we are talking about Innovation Infrastructure, we aren't talking about Google Fiber and wet labs, although those are elements that can be helpful. And we aren't just talking about assisted bike lanes and pop-up parks, although those can be nice and certainly help a place project a certain image. But those things are just bits of the system, not the whole.

Instead **Innovation Infrastructure is the intentionally interrelated, mutually-reinforcing system of activities, places, organizations, businesses and people that have the collective effect of accelerating innovation across the full spectrum of human activity.** That last phrase is also important - critically important, not just for good PR, but for innovators to be able to make the profound impact we all need them to create. More on that soon.

This rest of this book has three parts. The remainder of Part 1 orients us to the Big Issues that are driving the increase, the sometimes-effectiveness and the challenges facing innovation and entrepreneurship.

We'll also parse out the difference between innovation and entrepreneurship and explore the full scope of who needs to be innovating in our current and emerging economy. Using the infrastructure analogy, you can think of this as the topographic map that the engineers study to figure out where the pipes should run.[5]

Part 2 will give us a common language and a common understanding of the challenges inherent with the infrastructure as we have it today. We will define the elements that one might find in a fully formed Innovation Infrastructure, and how the pieces can (and sometimes, don't) fit together. You can think of this as the diagram of the existing system, showing the width of the roads and the turning radii of the intersections so that we can see where the existing design may cause problems.

In Part 3 we will turn our attention to the big question: **what do we need to do to accelerate innovation?** When we get to this point, we will focus our attention on the two elements that are mostly likely to drive a fully-effective Innovation Infrastructure: Innovation Districts and Entrepreneurship Ecosystems. And as we flesh out what a more impactful Innovation Infrastructure will do, we will focus in on Districts specifically. That's because their mix of physical space

---

[5] If you are an *actual* electric or civil or traffic engineer, please keep in mind that most readers of this book... aren't. Please accept my apologies for making it sound easier than it is or otherwise not exactly describing the correct process. I'm over-simplifying for sake of the analogy...and because I am assuming you don't want to read an AASHTO manual right now, either. Thanks.

and existing supporters provides the best available environment in which to envision a fully effective Innovation Infrastructure.

Throughout this book, you will find a very intentional focus on broad inclusion and diversity among Innovation Infrastructure participants. Let me be blunt: we insist that effective Innovation Infrastructure necessitates that the participants, the people who are doing the innovating, represent as much of the full broad range of human experience as we can get. An Innovation Ecosystem that is dominated by white men doing tech, or medical PhD's, or people who want to open bakeries, is not going to succeed enough, or achieve enough, or innovate enough to truly create the solutions that we all need them to create.[6] That's not a statement of idealism, or a political philosophy, but a statement of pragmatism: we need a lot to happen, fast, and the best way we know to accelerate innovation is through intentional diverse interactions. Given the economy we are moving into and the challenges we face in doing that successfully, we all need more than ever to learn from others who do not look or sound or think like us. That may be the strongest inherent argument for investing in Innovation Infrastructure: encountering and learning from and working with

---

[6] That doesn't mean at all that historically disadvantaged populations don't need additional support, or a place to find their footing outside of the trumpeting herd of the dominant culture. They most certainly do. And as we'll discuss in Part III, creating those kinds of spaces is some Program's greatest contribution. But that's not enough. No Program should be satisfied with just making its specific brand of participants feel happy. We need these Programs to help launch them into the larger Infrastructure, where they can discover new opportunities and help others see what they have been blinded to. A lot of times, we've been too timid to do that. That needs to change.

people who are different from us may be the most crucial element of our success, and it seems to be one of the hardest things for us to develop on our own. We build infrastructure to help us do the things we can't do in isolation, and unlocking our full innovative potential is no exception.

The Challenge: Innovation Worth Investing in Today

One of the most Captain Obvious statements I could make at near the beginning of this book is the following:

The world is changing.

I'll give you a moment to get done with your eye rolls.

We don't really know what to call the economic and social era that we are currently moving into yet. The Digital Age seems too tech-exclusive. The Network Age sounds like a Chamber of Commerce event. The Information Age doesn't seem to differentiate enough.

 The World Economic Fund gave it the catchy name of the Fourth Industrial Revolution, but for that to work you have to know what the previous three were and not get hung up on the idea that industrial = smokestacks. Which not everyone does.

Personally, I like the term "Fusion Age," for reasons that will become clear, but naming it after a technology that no one has gotten to work yet has some understandable branding problems.

For me, the most important thing to focus on in this new moment isn't computers or renewable energy in themselves, but the **emerging new opportunities to draw value from dispersed but synced resources**. It's a fundamental and profound shift in how the ability to get something - anything - done is organized. We have frequently framed these changes in terms of the internet, but the more profound implications manifest in everything from flash mob protests to disaster-resistant supply chain management.

Here's a fully incomplete snapshot of the most profound economic, scientific and societal trends underlying our changing world - not only our debates about Twitter and education and artificial intelligence, but about how we go about the work of creating and acting on new ideas. This isn't enough to even scratch at the variations and range of impact, but it's hopefully enough to get us all on the same page.

- We are moving from a world where linear projections seemed to work (or, at least, they were the closest we could get and when they missed it didn't seem to matter too much) to a necessity of understanding **multiple possibilities**.

  We find more and more that we can't realistically assume a given outcome, and we have to design our systems and lives around an expectation of uncertainty. For an example of this, think about the fact that the average job tenure is 3 to 4.5 years[7], and young workers are expected to have 12 to 15 different jobs in their lifetime[8].

- We are seeing a decline in the impact of conventional types of authoritativeness and a rise in what we might call **unmediated or non-dominant information alternatives** (I learn about an unfolding event from the scatter of the Twitter feed, not Walter Cronkite or NBC Nightly News).

- We are seeing a new kind of **power coming out of loose networks**, dispersed systems, showing its strength every time we have a Kickstarter launch or an online protest. This trend often faces opposition, and the old systems are holding on as hard as they can, but there's a definite shifting of the sands under any claim to be an expert.

- We seem to be seeing an **increasing awareness of the effects of**

---

[7]https://www.thebalancecareers.com/how-long-should-an-employee-stay-at-a-job-2059796

[8]https://www.linkedin.com/.../how-many-jobs-average-person-have-his-her-lifetime-scott...

interdependencies -- a dawning realization that policy decisions in China or damage to a fishery in the Atlantic or a mistake at a warehouse that I didn't know was in the next town over can have a direct effect on my own life. Again, that's incomplete, for the paradigm shift reasons I'll unpack shortly, but interdependence awareness seems to be seeping into the general awareness in a way that it has not before

None of these are entirely new, and none of them are fully understood and internalized all over (and some people outright resist these forces). Some of them are only coming to our awareness now because we were comfortable enough to ignore them before. But regardless of your political or social leanings, your economic theory, your technology love or hatred, it would be hard for a cogent person to not notice that some very fundamental things are changing.

So, within that macro-context, how do we innovate?

What does it mean to innovate?

Finding an all-inclusive definition for a term that has become ubiquitous in its poorly-defined-ness is... only slightly easier that defining that thing in the last section. Every writer, pundit and talking head expert can give you a definition of innovation, and some of them are actually coherent.

The definitions that have appeared to find the most use in the broadest range of contexts seem to have two core components:

- They involve something *new*...at least new to those on the receiving end of it.
- They *add value* for someone affected by it. And that value, as a corollary, can be *measured.*

OK, that's easy enough. Everybody like new things, and everybody likes things that add value. Opposing innovation would be like opposing puppies and kittens. Even if you don't want one yourself, most humans would say there's nothing inherently bad about those sweet little faces.

And innovation certainly isn't unique to the Fusion Era, of course. Innovations, per that definition, define most of the arc of history. And even systematic for-profit innovation isn't new: Thomas Edison's Menlo Park employed hundreds to develop, test, review and refine a slew of new products.

So the idea of innovating is not at all innovative itself. It's a part of what we've been doing for millenia.

Then why are we having such a hard time of it?

The Sputtering Innovation Machine

From a technology standpoint, writers often argue that the pace of innovation is accelerating exponentially, *a la* Moore's Law and its insistence that information processing technology will follow that growth curve. At the same time, however, writers in the business sphere, following the thread of Tyler Cowen's *Great Stagnation*, assert that innovation, or at least the incremental value of innovations, is declining. In making that case, many point to long-term declining numbers of patents and new business starts. Others argue that, while worrisome, those trends are at best very rough proxies for the full scope of innovation.

It's as much a definition problem as anything. Increasing information technology, we would think, should *inherently* provide value (and thus qualify as Innovation), but if no one is ready to use that value yet, is it actually Innovative? If a patent is granted, but it's for a slight tweak to a device that makes a small improvement to its existing function, is that actually innovation, or just twiddling at the edges?

But even if we admit that the answer to this question depends on your filter and your definitions, there does seem to be a general sense that innovation and entrepreneurship need improvement - or at least a decent goosing. For all of the years that the concept of Innovation as a business book category or a nonprofit mantra has been floating around, to the point where not a few of you probably have an innovation-fatigue reaction every time you read that word, it seems like it's not happening. At least not happening enough.

As Johann Wong of the innovation consulting firm JouleWatt says, "there are good things happening, but they're not happening or growing fast enough."

And in speaking to innovators ranging from investment firms to corporate products to public policy, you get the same sense: something is blocking us from achieving what we're truly capable of -- of truly capitalizing on all those new information processors and communication systems and all the *work* that's been invested from all sectors in the name of increasing Innovation.

So what's blocking us?

The Paradigm Shift

During one of my summers in college I worked for an office temp agency, on a series of stints that mostly involved using my magical capability to use WordPerfect to type up handwritten letters and the like (if you have no idea what I'm talking about, ask someone really old). I was bored out of my head and literally read anything I could get. Through this process, a Secondary Education major with a concentration in English found Thomas Kuhn's *Structure of Scientific Revolutions*, the book that introduced the concept of a **paradigm shift**. I wouldn't have known it then, but trying to stay awake those afternoons waiting for the next internal memo began me on a quest I couldn't have imagined:

How to get around one's own mental blind spots.

You may have read that book, but it's probably been a long time. So here's the synopsis: in examining how key scientific discoveries had developed through history, Kuhn noted that the most significant breakthroughs came about when someone who was not embedded in the prevailing thinking system was able to see (in some cases, literally) things that others could not. It wasn't any magic gift on the part of the innovator -- no x-ray glasses or abnormal intelligence or anything.

The innovator was able to innovate because the **existing assumptions and expectations around the topic blocked the prevailing "experts" from being able to see the new interpretation or new solution**. Sometimes those blockages came from straightforward articles of faith, sometimes they were unwritten and unspoken assumptions, and sometimes they were simply doubts or inklings that the experts avoided looking at because speaking what they thought they had seen would cost them their prestige, their livelihood, maybe more.

In all of the cases that Kuhn examined, evidence pointing to the new discovery had been around before the paradigm-breaker came on the scene. It had just been discounted, avoided, overlooked, misinterpreted, sometimes suppressed. The paradigm-breaker didn't see something no one else had ever seen. He or she *saw something about it that no one else had seen.*

In my own professional life, I have moved between a wider range of sectors than a lot of people. I've worked with large and small businesses, nonprofits, governments, lone wolf innovators, corporate lifers, you name it. And because I've done that, I've had to confront fundamentally different paradigms over and over again. That doesn't mean that I do a better job of getting myself out of my own way when *I* am on the inside of the paradigm, but it does mean that I've at least gotten accustomed to the idea that different paradigms lead to different world views and different assumptions about how to solve problems.

When you are the one who comes in from outside, you realize pretty quickly that the **"we've *Always* done it that way, why would you even think of doing anything else?" assertion in one place is the unimagined, totally novel idea in another**. Sometimes you look like the genius or the psycho just because you brought in an idea that's become the normal mode of operation somewhere else.

I think the great challenge facing innovators and those who want to accelerate innovation -in any space or industry or sector - is in understanding, taking apart and rebuilding the paradigms in which we are trying to create meaningful innovation. We have to get ourselves out of our own way, and since the paradigms that I think are causing most of our problems are so pervasive, we have few easy opportunities to bring in someone who can truly see what's outside of the box we have trapped ourselves in.

At least, within our current paradigm, it's hard to find those people. But that's a trap of our paradigm in itself. More on that later.

The Industrial-Fusion Age Innovation Clash

Despite our tablets and open offices and general lack of steam engines and child labor, the paradigms that surrounds our attempts at innovation are, at their core, Industrial Era systems. We think about work and creativity and how people relate to their work within the same structure of fundamental assumptions and expectations that governed the people who built cotton gins and Model T's. Business pundits tout ways to innovate, but most treat syStems for increasing innovation as bolt-ons, things to attach to the existing systems. The fundamental structure, too often, remains exactly the same.

That creates a mismatch, like trying to put an electric engine in a 1900s locomotive. The intakes and outputs are almost guaranteed not to line up right, and your jerry-rigs and modifications have a good chance of putting more strain on the system than it experienced before. And when that strain gets too severe and the old boiler risks blowing, your innovations are what's going to end up in the weeds beside the tracks.

Industrial- era organizations are designed to meet the objectives of industrial era systems. And bolting on a shiny innovation probably won't work, because the thing that threatens the integrity of the Industrial-era machine is the thing that will be eventually rejected, regardless of its novelty or promised long-term benefits.

At the core, our innovation systems and our rewards have been bolted on to the industrial era model, and the unresolved mismatch with these parts of the old paradigm create unending strain on everyone:

- **We value specialization, when what the new system needs is generalism**. Dermatologists make more money than general practitioners. Chief Finance Officers seldom lack a CPA or CFA. We tell our children to get "practical" degrees, and to go to graduate school so that their training aligns with the specific thing they think they want to do. That's a central legacy of the division of labor inherent in the industrial model.

  We know from our own life experience that a dermatologist probably won't catch my potentially-fatal heart disease, and that a set of letters don't guarantee that someone can complete a given task, and that careers change more quickly than they ever have. And if you read business press, you have probably seen articles about how tech companies are now seeking liberal arts graduates. But our paradigm still assumes each professional role will fit into a larger machine right where it's supposed to be, and stay there, like the mid-20th century assembly line worker who spent years tightening the same bolt on the same spot on the chassis of every machine that rolled by.

- **We default to command and control, when our technologies demand decentralized decision-making.** Conventional businesses, even those who have "flattened" their hierarchies over the past 20 years, still make most decisions by passing proposals through higher and higher levels of review and sign-off, until either an ultimate level of approval is achieved or the proposal is killed. Command and control protects the integrity of the system by rejecting new ideas that could possibly post a threat. But it's those threats that we often need most if we're going to actually make the big steps.

A couple of years ago, online retailer Zappos, already known for its unique approach to corporate culture, decided to radically decentralize its decision-making by implementing Holacracy - a highly structured organization model that eliminates all hierarchy and delegates nearly all decision-making to carefully designed systems of circles and areas of ownership across all of the employees. Zappos did this because they feared becoming disrupted - that a new online retailer without the baggage of their hierarchical review and decision process could take their market share and send them the way of Sears. They wanted to maintain flexibility, the ability to sense and react to changes in the market, to strengthen their ability to adapt in an unpredictable environment. It was an aggressive response, but it made foresighted sense in the light of the speed at which retail is changing

Nearly 30% of employees left within the first year.[9] Those who left came from nearly every level and job description in the previous model - an indicator of how much even employees of a nontraditional company had internalized the industrial age business model. For some employees, the prospects of greater company health and personal engagement could not overcome their deep-seated adherence to the command and control model.

- **We understand transaction math but don't know how to quantify mutual benefit.** One of the emerging and seemingly self-evident

---

[9] In keeping with the longtime Zappos approach, people who left were offered what is typically described as a "generous" buyout package, to further ensure that people who are not committed to the culture don't stay for financial reasons.

principles of a network economy is that each participants' livelihood is intrinsically interdependent on the rest of the system.

Unlike the Rockefeller-type Industrial-era megaliths, who could control every part of their process from mining to part stamping, most modern businesses of any size are reliant on their ability to tap into the network. Even a behemoth like Amazon captures its value from connecting and organizing the presentation of thousands of individual suppliers. It doesn't print the books and make the things it sells all by itself.

The term "ecosystem" first entered business parlance through networks of small software startups. These micro-companies relied on the ecosystem for as much as they possibly could - shared co-working space, specialist contractors, support services like marketing, and more.

The expectation - which seemed radical through the eyes of a Rockefeller - was that the business did not have to "own" everything. It could tap into the ecosystem when needed to purchase only what it required. For computer chip makers, owning a silicon mine looks liked lunacy, although that would have been the assumption about how to run a big business 100 years ago.

But *when mutual benefit ecosystems get measured in terms of transactions, their value is substantially understated.* Because no one "owns" the latent potential of the ecosystem, it remains off the economic ledger - except for specific transactions, which are a fraction of the ecosystem's total value. Traditional economics simply doesn't account for it well.

And what we don't measure, we don't value.

This happens at the micro level, when a young network business struggles to demonstrate its value in transactional terms, despite the fact that its existence provides a crucial on-demand resource for other businesses. And it happens at the macro level, when policy makers default to big business incentives over investing in the startup ecosystem because the first one is a straightforward and (presumably) predictable transaction. And the numbers look a lot bigger.

- **We prize efficiency over flexibility.** Flexibility requires redundancy - the ability to fall back on an alternative system or funding source or person when Plan A falls through. But efficiency has been the watchword of the Industrial Era, symbolized by the assembly line precision and Six Sigma process evaluations. In the traditional assembly line, each movement, each micro-step, even the placement of each part storage bin is precisely choreographed, with no margin for improvisation. Which is why most traditional assembly line roles today are filled by robots. And which is also why an error at one station shuts down the whole line. In a traditional assembly line, there are no work-arounds.[10]

As Nassim Taleb so clearly articulated, highly efficient systems are inherently fragile - if one part goes out of alignment, the entire machine falls down. Which is why economies crash over obscure mortgage bundling schemes, or why power goes out across multiple states due to a cascade that started with one tree sagging onto the wrong power line. When everything is precisely, efficiently, optimally connected, redundancy gets cut - it was redefined as waste.

An ecosystem lives or dies by its redundancies. When the forest fire burns, trees release their seeds to lay the groundwork for the new growth. When climate change makes a habitat inhospitable for one creature, another may move into that niche. When a store in a

---

[10] If you are familiar with manufacturing, you probably know that very few factories or plants actually use the traditional assembly line process described here anymore - instead, highly-trained people work in teams or cells to manage the process as it unfolds, using their expertise to check and test and problem-solve in the middle of the process. The challenge for us is that people who don't work in manufacturing don't often know how it has changed, and their mental image of an efficient manufacturing process still looks like a Model T plant.

commercial district goes out of business, other astute business owners may notice increased demand for a product as consumers look for a new option, and stock more of the thing they are seeking. A system that can manage the inevitable shocks and setbacks without falling apart has a change of returning to equilibrium, and even growing. But that requires a reasonable level of redundancy.

- **We create complex systems, forgetting that this makes them fragile, not resilient.** This idea is also embedded in the assembly line efficiency concept, but it's worth digging into the question of how complexity inherently leads to fragility.

  How we manage land use is a good example. When zoning laws were first created in the early 1900s, and through the 1970s, the primary principle used to decide how land should develop was *separation of uses* -- factories should be away from residences, commercial should be closer to residential but not too close, etc.

  This was feasible as long as one was zoning never-developed farm fields, but most places with existing factories and houses and commercial already had some intermingling. We dealt with this by creating more and more layers of complexity - first non-conforming uses to sequester those old factory neighborhoods, then setbacks and floor area ratios and landscape requirements to make new construction match the existing environment (or a longed-for, upgraded future), then overlays and performance objectives and special incentives zones to tweak the process in one way or another.

Every community is different, but these attempts to standardize through complexity often created three sets of unanticipated opportunities for the system to break:

- Understanding of the zoning process becomes limited to a very few, both within government agencies and outside. This means that the process of determining a change to permitted land use (for example, when a proposed business does not explicitly fit the permitted land use categories) becomes dominated by expensive experts. As a result, reusing older properties for new uses can become even harder, especially for potential business owners who cannot afford legal fees.

- The lack of clarity around what is permitted and what kind of change is possible exacerbates land use conflicts, Since most people cannot decipher the code to understand for themselves, they may find themselves blindsided by a permissible land use that they didn't know was possible.

- The accretion of tweaks and overlays and amendments over time can create conflicts within the code itself. It's not unusual for two points of code to indicate conflicting preferred land uses or setback standards or landscape requirements when applied to a specific parcel, although those regulations might have made sense by themselves.

And when any of these breaks occur, the cost in time and money, broken trust and frustration, and loss of faith in the larger system, can easily outlast the approval process.

- **We treat externalities as far more external than they actually are.** In classic economics, externalities are a kind of accounting trick: since the core focus is on the specifics of a transaction, an "externality" is an outcome of the transaction that doesn't show up on the balance sheet for either party. When the transaction results in something that neither the supply nor the demand side value, it's called an "externality" and tossed aside.

Except that tossing it aside doesn't make it go away.

Before I was born, my father and my grandfather operated a small paint factory. They bought the ingredients, made the paint, canned it and sold it to companies that used in on their machinery, their buildings, their streets. But sometimes something went wrong with the making of the paint -- an ingredient was off, someone put the wrong thing in by accident, someone misunderstood what the customer wanted and made the wrong thing. This was before environmental regulations.

When that happened.... They dumped it in the woods behind the factory. An externality. Problem solved. Except that those chemicals and rusting cans are still leaching into the creek at the bottom of the hill decades later.

Environmental regulations that make businesses responsible for their toxic waste were established to force those costs back into the supply/demand equation. Without those requirements - especially when you have a defunct company where all the owners are dead - those "externalities" become someone else's problem. In many cases, they become everyone's problem. To the people affected by what the buyer or seller did not want, those chemicals are not "externalities" at all.

Most of the most significant limitations of an industrial era mindset and systems in this Fusion economy come down to the fact that *depending more on a network and less on ourselves means that externalities are no longer externalities at all.* If it affects the network, it will affect us, one way or another. Even when we persist in the industrial mindset, our resistance doesn't change the fact that we are increasingly dependent on these interdependencies.

None of the paradigm clashes in the list above are obscure, or require specialized knowledge, or constitute some kind of inside ball, incomprehensible to anyone but a few high priests. And that's the point.

We know in our guts, just from what goes on around us, that our existing systems are coming up short in meeting these emerging challenges. We are acutely aware of our need for something fundamentally new, but we can't see what those new systems really look like yet. So, to use the old saying, we too often stick with the devil we know, even when the clashes threaten to overwhelm us.

Industrial-Age thinking meets Fusion-Age Innovation

One of the big implications of this paradigm clash falls squarely on our methods for enabling innovation. Because of the barriers we discussed above, we too often find ourselves hamstrung, stuck with under-effective efforts because we don't have a way to do anything else.

Let's take this sector by sector, looking at who we conventionally think of as active "innovators"... and perhaps a few that you don't.

Big Companies. Business students can usually list a number of big businesses who are innovation leaders in their industry...3M, Procter & Gamble, Apple, etc. We hear them praised for putting very intentional work into innovation, and for good reason. While most companies anymore tout "innovation" in their missions and marketing materials, some are clearly more refined and systematic in their innovation than others. But when you spend time with innovators within these and other companies, a few common points of hamstringing occur:

- **Sequestering.** In many big businesses, innovation is done within a separate, set-apart group - what Lockheed Martin famously called a "Skunkworks." In other words, the innovators have some special magic, and everyone else is just supposed to keep to their knitting.

That might have been beneficial during World War II, but as we will discuss throughout this book, we're convinced that true innovation requires engaging the most diverse range of experiences and perspectives we can get in a process of solving for a solution. What might the Skunkworks have been able to invent if they could embed the builders and users of their technology right into its development?

- **Rewards.** At large companies, promotion and salary increases are commonly linked to the value that an employee's product or line of business created over the past year. The path to advancement and raises, therefore, runs through the largest volume parts of the business - typically *not* the products that are open to a whole lot of disruption. Laboring in the innovation sub-basement may have other benefits that don't show up in the yearly review process, but in most mainstream businesses it seems to be extra hard to get from the skunkworks to a corner office.

- **Danger of the borderlands.** It's not a surprise to anyone who follows innovation that the most interesting things happen when you combine perspectives - when you bring the tools of one industry into another's context, when you create something that combines the best of two products into one uniquely new item. But working on that within a larger company can mean to put yourself outside the silo walls, in the organization's no-man's-land.

Who are you reporting to (and does she/he know anything about the other kind of product)? Who is paying the expenses? Who gets credit if it's a win? Whose brand do we put on it? Whose profit center owns it? Do they want to do it, or are they uncomfortable with something that isn't their core product? Questions like these can put not only the project, but one's career, at risk.

- **Starving in the middle of the field.** People outside of a BigCo often assume that anything you're working on will have a nice, fat budget. But a good project can starve simply because it's not important enough to anyone to advocate for it. And unlike in small business, options for alternative funding are tightly constrained -if the innovation does not fit within one of three budget lines in the right department, it could have no other choice but to die.

None of this is to bash BigCos. Most are led by well-intentioned people who do want to seek progress. But, like any paradigm, once you are embedded in it, it's hard to imagine working differently.

The unfortunate side-effect is that innovation in most BigCos fights with one hand tied behind its back. What potential benefits, not just for the company but for everyone, might be possible if innovation happened within a system that rewarded and leaned into the resources of a Fusion economy?

Universities. To the non-university public, colleges sometimes look like lands of grand exploration and exciting discoveries, but the process of taking a lab discovery to market through a university typically involves as much bureaucracy, sequestering, reward misalignment, borderlands danger and starvation risk as any BigCo. Innovation and tech transfer systems within a university are designed with an eye to capturing as much of the value of a discovery as possible for the university system (they have, after all, provided the labs and offices). So while there may be systems for moving IP to market, raising the university's innovation reputation in the community, and establishing some joint ventures or special programs, these systems can create as many roadblocks to innovation as they enable.

As with the BigCos, the challenge hamstringing university innovation lies at the root: universities conceive of the innovation process as something that happens entirely and exclusively within the walls of the factory, and not as part of a larger distributed ecosystem. They may see benefits to collaborating with industry and entrepreneurs, but the systems designed to protect the image and standing and economics of the university can create as many barriers as any BigCo.

Nonprofit organizations face similar industrial era / fusion era misalignments, often with poor results for those who have the most urgent needs. In addition to the risks of borderlands, reward misalignment, and the others we have discussed, here's a few structural industrial era leftovers that particularly hamstring nonprofits trying to innovate.

- Nonprofits are, almost by default, defined as existing on some alternative plane from businesses. Nonprofits often earn some portion of their total revenue from services, classes, product sales etc., but for U.S. nonprofits in particular, demonstrating a significant amount of income from sales can trigger a review of whether they are truly nonprofit. For this reason (and like many things, the perceived risk often outweighs the actual risk), most nonprofits depend on charitable funders, including foundations, wealthy donors, and government programs.

  But nonprofits can easily find themselves **contorting their mission and their programs** to meet a funder's criteria -and those criteria can be very rigid, especially in their application and documentation requirements. Like innovators within BigCos, finding new funding opportunities if the usual suspects don't fit can mean starving an innovation for lack of ability to find a new way, like selling a service or serving a different audience, if doing so will jeopardize the funder relationship.

- The core assumption of a nonprofit being outside of the conventional (industrial era) business system also means that nonprofits are **assumed to be somehow less vital, less relevant** to the core operation of a business or community than a for-profit business. "Charity" implies supplemental, additional, a bolt-on, a luxury. Since charities largely deal in the externalities created by the industrial-era economy, the Industrial-era system assumes that the value of their work is less than that of "real" business.

This part of the paradigm has a lot of unfortunate impacts on nonprofits, including lousy pay and a tendency to be treated disparagingly by business leaders. But there's a significant, and problematic, unintended consequence that may constrain a nonprofit's ability to innovate even further.

This dismissive message from the for-profit sector, coupled with a history of being asked to apply ill-fitting business impact measures to their work, has created an prevalence of distrust from nonprofits toward any for-profit model. The popularity of the blog Nonprofit AF points to this frustration, with its frequent illumination of the effects of typical funder requirements, such as unreasonable impact metric systems, on small and diverse nonprofits.

This disconnect from the prevailing economy leads to not only a decreased sense of nonprofit self-worth, but an unfortunate tendency to procure poor quality goods and services that do not enhance the organization's capacity as much as it needs. In this context, living hand-to-mouth becomes the only option, and the ability to innovate at all, despite the desperate urgency of the needs the organization sees every day, is stifled.

Governments, especially local governments, face particularly difficult barriers to innovation because of their unique role in modern (read: Industrial-era) society. More so in this era than any previous, governments became responsible for protecting the public interest: the historic police power expanded to include the provision of public water and sewer systems, building codes, equal housing regulations and more.

For an increasingly urbanizing society, this proliferation of specialized roles was necessary, but it led to the development of a model of administration that decentralized most decision-making, requiring the new bureaucrat to confine her or his role to their specific expertise, like the assembly line worker. It also distributed political power among a wider array of elected and appointed officials, as well as frequently overlapping governmental agencies.

The resulting governance was more stable but more slow to change, more professional but less intrinsically able to adapt to evolutions in technology, economy or culture. Local governments in the United States today struggle with massive disconnects between how value is generated and how 19th century tax programs were established, between systems designed to make sure all got treated fairly and demands to address inequities, between public participation systems set up for classically-trained 19th century white men and the array of people and cultures who find it necessary to participate in local government today.

Efforts to innovate government have accelerated in the past 10 years, in congruence with similar efforts in business, and several larger US, Canadian and other cities have found creative ways to enact beneficial changes. But, just like the innovators in BigCos, government innovators find that they are subject to borderland risks, sequestering limits, misaligned rewards and more. And the public visibility of those mismatched legacy structures means that changing them involves a special level of difficulty and risk.

So what happens to innovation and entrepreneurship programs, districts and ecosystems?

Given the last chapter and everything so far in this one, it's no surprise that the way the Industrial / Fusion Economy clash plays out has a big impact on the programs and systems we develop to try to advance innovation.[11] From various perspectives, you can see the structural challenges inherited from each of the previous sectors playing out in your favorite innovation initiative. Here's a few common ones:

- **Limited and ineffective strategies for picking "winners."** A large number of programs for innovators and entrepreneurs give out a most-likely-to-succeed award, whether through a prize at completion, a demanding selection process, a project contract or another means of designating the top of the top. However, we have little evidence to indicate whether we are actually picking the most likely to succeed or not, and much anecdotal evidence to indicate that in a lot of cases, we are probably far off the mark. We assume, in other words, that we can command-and-control the innovation process, and there are significant questions as to whether that's actually the case..

---

[11] Later in this book, Programs, Districts and Ecosystems will take on specific definitions that we will use from that point on. Here I am using those more generically, which is why I didn't list all five of the Pumps.

One of the metrics often used to judge the viability of startup or innovation program participants are the opinions of venture capital investors -- even though less than 1% of all startups see venture capital funding[12] and there is substantial evidence to indicate that most venture capitalist don't actually make such great choices.[13] But we defer to the presumed experts because that is the Industrial Era way.

- **Utility agnosticism.** For most accelerators, incubators and similar programs, questioning an applicant regarding the conventional market potential of their product is *de rigueur.* Questioning whether the offering will create significant new *value* in the market doesn't happen as often as it should (the likelihood that your neighborhood *needs* a new cupcake shop is pretty slim.)

  And questioning whether the product will actually improve the world -- allow people to do something substantially new, address a significant barrier to quality of life, tackle one of

---

[12] "Trends in Venture Capital, Angel Investments, and Crowdfunding across the Fifty Largest U.S. Metropolitan Areas: Annual Survey of Entrepreneurs Data Briefing Series" Dane Stangler, Inara S. Tareque, and Arnobio Morelix. December 2016

[13] For a fascinating deep dive into the actual financial mechanics of venture capital, check out "The meeting that showed me the truth about VCs" by Tomer Dean, published in Techcrunch on June 1, 2017: https://techcrunch.com/2017/06/01/the-meeting-that-showed-me-the-truth-about-vcs/

the significant challenges facing a community - we don't ask that much.

As a result, pitch nights end up laced with businesses that promise great money-making opportunities from applying a new technology to...sell more stuff to people who don't need it or want it. Or address a minor need of some highly privileged market segment.

There's no reason why people shouldn't be able to start whatever business they want to, whether grand or incremental in scope. But the fact that we don't make that distinction, even when scarce public or charitable funds are being spent, indicates that we are thinking in conventional Industrial Era terms. Benefits that fall outside of a profit/loss sheet have no value - they are *externalities* - and that means that they cannot be accounted as part of "rational" or "responsible" decision-making around the viability of a new businesses.

So, Industrial Era-wise, we cannot differentiate between a business that will have a needed Fusion Era network impact, and those that won't. Even though, as we will discuss shortly, when the stakes of *not* impacting those externalities are higher than ever.

- **Lack of systemic critical analysis and adjustment.** In dealing with new businesses and innovators, most programs coach people to take some variant of a lean or agile approach - make prototypes, test, study the results, make revisions, test again. But few programs truly do the same: they may do a "strategic plan" every two or three years, but that looks more like a conventional nonprofit task than an agile discovery process. As a result, few startup or innovation organizations actually operate like startups or innovators themselves.

One of the biggest risks of not following a lean process is that unexamined assumptions, or unspoken expectations, are allowed to perpetuate unchallenged. The magical thinking behind the "Collision" theory of innovation - that innovation will occur in places where bright people somehow bump into each other and discover what the other is interested in - is a good example of how an untested hypothesis becomes accepted as an article of faith and a basis for investing in real estate.

To my knowledge, no one has verified that the presence of collision-friendly spaces increases innovation, but entire districts have been built around this assumption. Meanwhile, the research that has been conducted seems to indicate that people seldom spontaneously "collide" with people that they don't already know or don't already have strong similarities.[14] The collision effect turns out to be much weaker

---

[14] https://hbr.org/2018/07/the-other-diversity-dividend

than expected, and the potentially transformative impacts of rich diversity of thought, perspective, insight, continue to go untapped.

The result? Similar to what we described with BigCos: too much of the system's innovative potential is squandered. We are essentially limiting our innovators to the model of work and problem-solving that defined the last era, not the one into which we are moving.

When inadequate innovation isn't enough

So the complaints I am levelling against our current innovation systems are that they're working from an old model that doesn't fit the world that is emerging - a world that isn't quite here yet.

So what?

Every major change in how we live and work, you might argue, goes through a transition period. Early personal computers looked like a typewriter attached to a TV. Home heating had to move from the open fireplace through the pot-bellied stove before we could get to forced-air furnaces that work without us having to put wood in them. The first automobiles didn't look like Corvettes or Civics -- they looked almost identical to the things that horses were pulling, except that there was no horse.

So calm down. We'll get there. What's the rush?

Here's the short version of why we don't have the luxury of waiting: the externalities of the Industrial Era have piled up, are piling up deep, and if we don't accelerate the speed at which we are addressing them, we're all going to be in trouble.

That's not tinfoil hat talk. That's not alarmist Chicken Little language. It's the logical conclusion of a clear-eyed look at the worldwide data in front of us.

For a concise and well-informed overview of the core challenges facing the globe in the next 10 to 20 years, take a look at the United Nations Development Programme's Sustainable Development Goals (SDGs). This framework of the SDGs was designed to guide international investment, but in the process, they give us a fact-driven insight into the core challenges facing humanity in this time. Some, like poverty, are age-old issues at their roots, but have been exacerbated in many places by globalization, environmental damage, climate change, etc. Others are relatively new to our consciences, historically speaking, like equitable opportunities for women.

Take a look at this sampling of statistics from the SDGs [15] to get a sense of the global scope:

- Every day in 2014, an average of 42,000 people had to abandon their homes due to conflict.
- Children born into poverty are almost twice as likely to die before the age of 5 as those from wealthier families.
- 103 million youth worldwide lack basic literacy skills, and more than 60 percent of them are women.

[15] All of these statistics quoted are from http://www.undp.org/content/undp/en/home/sustainable-development-goals/

- Water scarcity affects more than 40 percent of the global population, and that figure is projected to rise.
- Energy is the dominant contributor to climate change, accounting for around 60 percent of global greenhouse gas emissions.
- 470 million jobs will be needed to absorb new entrants to the labour market between 2016 and 2030.
- More than 4 billion people still do not have access to the Internet
- At the current rate of progress, the World Economic Forum says it will take 217 years to close the gender gap in employment opportunities and pay.
- Cities occupy just 3 percent of the Earth's land but account for 60 to 80 percent of energy consumption and 75 percent of carbon emissions.
- 1.3 billion tons of food is wasted every year, while almost 2 billion people go hungry or undernourished.
- For each 1 degree Celsius of [average yearly] temperature increase, grain yields decline by about 5 percent.
- As much as 40 percent of the ocean is heavily affected by pollution, depleted fisheries, loss of coastal habitats and other human activities.
- Of the more than 80,000 tree species, less than one percent have been studied for potential use.
- Corruption, bribery, theft and tax evasion cost developing countries US$1.26 trillion per year.

A natural reaction for many of us is to respond to these statistics from a moral standpoint: *These things should not be!!!!* And there's nothing wrong with that. But for a moment, put on your Fusion Era Accountant green eyeshade:

How much value could you unlock by providing even a partial solution to any one of these? How much would that be worth?

Under an Industrial Era model, most of these issues were externalities, not accounted for in the economic operations of the world, so not the concern of businesses. They fell into that nonprofit or government bucket, which means that they were always treated as incidental to creating value. But we've said the the Fusion Era is being defined by a dependence on human creativity, reliance on networked webs of resources, and an increasing awareness of interdependence. All of these statistics above, and many more, indicate a big threat to those value-generators.

And deflecting a threat is usually one of the most effective ways to generate value.

What kind of value to a Fusion Era economy would you create if you could make food that would otherwise be discarded into something that provides a value to others - especially since discarding becomes increasingly expensive when cities are dense and energy costs a lot?

What kind of new products could you create if you could organize unemployed youth to provide something of value to the Fusion Era economy, perhaps by creating new products that meet the needs of the untapped global markets they know best?

How much value would you provide to not only citizens, but global corporations, if you could use technology to increase government transparency and make it more difficult for unscrupulous officials to demand bribes?

Given the potential value of solutions like these to the Fusion Economy, why would you build another dog-walking app, or a tool for selling more stuff to rich people, or any one of the mundane, slight-extension-of-something-else-to-the-same-demographics-that-we-already-overwhelm-with-advertising that too often dominates our innovation programs?

Let's be clear, though: Mundane and local are by no means the same thing. The communities that people live in and rely on and care about desperately need good local businesses of all descriptions. You can be addressing the local version of an SDG goal in the place that you care about, and that can be both valuable and worth doing. The challenge that the SDGs raise for locally-focused businesses is not necessarily to solve the world's problems, but to figure out how you can unlock new value for your community by constructively addressing an unmet Fusion Age need.

Businesses large and small are stepping up to this challenge, from mobile water filtration systems to products made by survivors of abuse. But at this point, these efforts are a drop in the bucket compared to what we need.

We need more innovation, a lot more innovation and we need it to happen as fast as it possibly can. Which means that we need to shift our innovation systems to the Fusion Age as quickly as humanly possible.

There is no *prima facie* reason why we shouldn't be able to develop truly groundbreaking solutions. We have the tools we need more than ever. But our slowness in moving on from the Industrial Age is blocking our way.

Who Needs To Innovate (Or, Are We Innovating or Entrepreneur....ing, and does it matter?)

When you look at a master catalogue of business books, chances are you will see two section names in the list, among the others:

> Innovation
> Entrepreneurship

Start reading the book summaries, you're likely to fund the following:

- *Innovation* books mostly focus on two related items: (1) processes and techniques for thinking innovatively or helping a group innovate, and (2) making innovation happen within a corporation. Innovation, it would appear from that shelf, is something mostly done by people within a larger organization.

- *Entrepreneurship* books are mostly geared toward existing and potential business founders. Entrepreneurship, you will be led to believe, is all about finding your personal vision/value/thing you care about/thing you think you can make some money off, and then doing the work to get you to that promised land.

As with the classifications that I will use later in this book, publishers treat these two topics as separate things because it makes it easier to understand (and set up search algorithms).

But doing that obscures the commonalities, shared needs, and potential synergies that our Innovation Infrastructure must have if it is to have the kinds of impact we all need.

Given the previous chapter about trends impacting our national and global need for accelerated innovation, let's think a bit about who needs to be innovating -- and for this I'm going to adapt what I found to be a very useful classification in Maria Meyers' and Kate Pope Hodel's *Beyond Collisions: How to Build Your Entrepreneurial Infrastructure,* while adding a few more to try to cover a few more categories that I think are important to our exploration.

Innovation-Led Businesses. *Beyond Collisions* describes these as companies that have "intellectual property that contributes to a strong competitive advantage in the marketplace and serves as a foundation for a high rate of growth." These are often the marquee players, especially in a university-led innovation district or a seed fund portfolio. They're the ones that are expected to Hit it Big. The name itself says that they're innovating, and they're in a book about entrepreneurship systems.

So what's the problem?

The kinds of innovation that the Innovation-Led leaders often know how to do is technical, specific -- design a portable high-capacity water filter, create a more efficient solar cell, invent an artificial intelligence application. Arguably, important stuff, and certainly worthy of calling Intellectual Property.

The challenge is that they may need even more innovation than they're doing. By the time they reach the stage where you can call them an "Innovation-Led Business," these organizations usually have at a plan for who they will sell to, how they will reach their market, etc. But what happens when Plan A falls apart? What happens when a marketing channel fails to work, a pilot contract gets cancelled, the next round of consumer feedback indicates that people don't want it as much as you though they would?

For Innovation-Led businesses, finding a Plan B that puts their IP to work requires a whole different kind of innovation - one that their leaders may not know how to do. While the star Innovation-Led businesses may be able to hire a pivot wizard (and they might get lucky and get someone who can actually do it), many that aren't on that stage yet see no option but to curl up and shrivel.

Second Stage businesses. Entrepreneurship thought leaders like the Edward Lowe Foundation are increasingly championing these more mature organizations - typically defined as growth-oriented businesses with ten to 100 employees and annual revenue in the low millions. And the help these businesses need is typically described as coaching and equipping leadership to manage high rates of growth.

Second Stage businesses may definitely need help growing their operations, but just because they have left the fledgling stage does not mean that they may not have an urgent need to innovate. A product that broke new ground three years ago may now have up-and-coming competitors. A hiring strategy that worked in the beginning may need a deep re-think to make it work better in a global market. A newly-discovered environmental risk or unethical practices of a supplier might require an extensive redesign of the supply chain using emerging contractors. And discovering that your product is beloved in a market you didn't even know existed might mean that the packaging or promotion of the item might need to completely change.

Main Street. These businesses are the local bedrock -- from coffee shops to repair garages. Often locally owned, often locally-invested, often overlooked. While some organizations, like the American Independent Business Alliance and National Main Street programs and their local affiliates advocate for these businesses, and while some training and support focuses on them (the CoStarters network being an international example), Main Street businesses often get left out of the most serious entrepreneurship support efforts - and out of most that have substantial funding. But with extensive data indicating that these businesses have more pound-for-pound impact on the local economy than anyone else[16], it's makes little sense to overlook them.[17]

Add on to that the fact that Main Street businesses are under more pressure - and have less help - to innovate than almost anyone else in this list. Street traffic retail is plummeting, even artisan goods can be bought a dozen or more places online, everything from payment technologies to advertising changes continuously, and conventional models for employee management, inventory, deliver and more fail to make sense for these businesses, given the new economy in which they find themselves.

If we want to have streets with filled storefronts, places for people who aren't wealthy to build a nest egg, places for people to eat and drink and meet and care about, we need Main Street businesses. And they need help figuring out how to innovate.

Microenterprise. Some programs describe these entrepreneurs as "freelancers," but I prefer this term because it does a better job of including non-office work, such as hairdressing, catering, lawn care, repairs, etc. Microenterprises very often get overlooked, especially by the more well-funded organizations[18] because they're not expected to have very much "impact." But there's evidence to indicate that

[16] https://www.amiba.net/resources/multiplier-effect/

[17] Full disclosure, at this writing, I am a board member of an AMIBA affiliate and a former Main Street program board member. I have nothing with the CoStarters folks, but I think they're cool.

[18] Another full disclosure: as of this writing, I am also a board member of a microenterprise -focused nonprofit. Resume download complete.

microentrepreneurs have significant overlooked impact, from sustaining a more flexible labor pool to supplementing family income to creating a path to employment for people who face barriers to conventional jobs.

A microentrepreneur's need for innovation support often stems from her limited experience. If a microentrepreneur's experience is limited to one neighborhood, or one type of product, or one socioeconomic level, it will be much harder for her to assess whether it makes sense to pursue opportunities in a different kind of market. Too many times, I've seen this end up in on one of two paths: the microentrepreneur gets into trouble trying to serve a market she doesn't understand, or she sticks with what's known and familiar and limited. For a microentrepreneur from a disadvantaged background, this second path may be less risky, but it increases the odds that she will struggle to make it work -- unless she finds some help figuring out an innovative way to address that market more efficiently.

Larger corporations, or BigCo. I added this one, and the next two -- *Beyond Collisions* is focused on entrepreneurship, so it naturally doesn't address them. But including a city or region's largest employers in an innovation acceleration strategy - not just as sponsors or visitors, but as actual hands-on participants - couldn't be more crucial to our long-term success.

When you look at a BigCo from the outside, it's easy to think that it has it all together - that whatever innovation its people need to do, whatever problems they need to solve, they've got enough money and brains to figure it out. But as we discussed previously that's very rarely the truth.

As we noted in the last chapter, BigCos are under enormous pressure to innovate - they know enough about their industry, and they've seen enough other BigCos falter, to realize that they have to get to the future, fast. But at the same time as they are seeing these trends, BigCos live within an organizational system that is intentionally designed to limit risk. So that puts our BigCo intrapreneurs, and their companies, in a very interesting place.

If you think that's their problem, something we should just leave alone, talk to someone who lived through the 1980s in Cleveland or Buffalo, or the Great Recession in Las Vegas. If you have the choice, you'd prefer not watch a few innovation-unsuccessful BigCos drag your community through that again.

Nonprofits and public institutions. Most cities and regions in North America are grappling with a combination of growing income inequality, concentrated poverty and an unravelling public safety net. This means that organizations that exist to serve the public good - from neighborhood food pantries to hospital networks - face an acute and growing demand for services. In many quarters, these organizations are finding that they are stuck in a nonprofit funding model, and the traditional funding sources are either drying up or demanding results that the conventional way of doing things isn't delivering. How do you get out of that catch-22 - especially when your leadership has always worked within that model?

Profound, more-than-surface-deep-innovation is a crucial need in the nonprofit world, and it's one that has proven especially hard to break through.

Government. No one in innovation or entrepreneurship seems to want to go anywhere near the government sector (except a dedicated tribe of self-termed government nerds associated with networks like Code For America).[19] But it's hard not to argue that governments need to innovate as much or more than anyone else. Some larger cities, including Boston, Philadelphia, Denver and others have made strides in innovating everything from permit processes to employee feedback, and some smaller cities, like Rockford, Illinois and Gary, Indiana, have found some creative ways to tackle tough challenges. But almost across the board, they need more help.

While it may be useful to have some activities focused on only one of these sectors, our usual approach of keeping them in their separate lanes - or declaring some "innovative" and others "entrepreneurial" - may mean we are shooting ourselves in the foot.

---

[19] OK, one more full disclosure: I used to edit an online digest called *Engaging Cities* that focused on government innovation and technology. I can assure you that #govtech and #civictech innovators are out there. I recommend you go find them.

At the end of the day, in this moment in time, we as a community, as a world, need every bit of innovation we can get. We need to evaluate what we're doing - whether it's cutting lawns or manufacturing detergent or running employment programs - and we need to be able to take them apart, figure out how they can work together and rebuild to fit what we think is coming.

No one of us is going to have all the tools we need by ourselves, so we're going to have to be ready to borrow, to learn from others who are different than ourselves.

Innovation in the coming era can't be about twiddling the edges, or doing more of what we already know. The forces we talked about in the last chapter mean that extrapolating the past into the future doesn't work any more, and that we need to find some new solutions....fast.

Part 2 will lay out some of the tools we currently have to work with, so that we can envision how to build the collective Innovation Infrastructure that we all need.

Part 2: Today's Innovation Infrastructure: Pumps and Pipes

Just because we are relatively new to creating innovation infrastructure does not mean that we haven't built a ton of pieces already – and even hooked up a lot of them. So to understand the infrastructure we will need to accelerate innovation, let's start by making sure we have a clear, shared understanding of the pieces we have constructed so far.

As we noted before, a shared classifications system is one of the building blocks of any kind of analysis. People working on innovation and entrepreneurship often find that the names for different types of activities change from one place to the next – for example, the term "E-ship" is used throughout the SourceLink network, which is concentrated in the Great Plains but includes programs across the U.S. Say that term to people outside of that network, however, and you may get a blank stare.

So we're going to start this section with five different types of individual organizations. To continue to extend our infrastructure metaphor, we'll refer to these as the Pumps -- the sources of the power that moves the larger system. Then we'll explore common ways that these Pumps interact with each other -- call that the Pipes. And then, of course, we will need to spend some time examining how the Pumps and Pipes often break down, misconnect, or otherwise don't do what they were intended to do.

The Pumps

Few things bedevil a writer more than trying to make sense of a multi-dimensional topic in the linear world of words and sentences. You have to start somewhere, but that somewhere is necessarily going to be incomplete - a partial sketch that leaves out, for the moment, crucial information that would make the picture 3-dimensional. This is the challenge of starting a description of Innovation Infrastructure with the kinds of discrete programs and buildings and the like that they include.

While this is the right place to start, if for no other reason than these are the things you can Google, focusing on the parts means that we momentarily ignore the connections. Those will be the topic of the next chapter, but even with that the importance of those connections are easy to overlook, because we cannot see them. We will have to make a conscious effort to hold onto the understanding that these Pumps do not, or at least should not, function in isolation.

As we noted in the introduction to this section, Innovation Infrastructure includes a wide variety of organizations, activities and places -- and the language we use to talk about them usually isn't standardized. So it makes sense to start by establishing some standardized language. We'll be using these terms:

- Programs
- Places
- Nerve Centers
- Districts
- Ecosystems

As you will see, some individual efforts will fall into more than one of these categories. A Place may host a Program, or the Program can be delivered across an Ecosystem. A District might have several Nerve Centers, and some Nerve Centers may offer their own Programs.

We will find less value in trying to wedge a specific organization's work into one of these categories than in using this structure to understand how various activities might fit into the larger system. As I found when I confronted my own mental barriers in trying to figure out how to do things differently in Econogy's early days, we need structures to help us think, but if we start treating them as rigid absolutes, we become blocked from important parts of what we should be learning.

Here's the terms we will be using:

Programs are specific activities or closely related groups of activities that are administered as a set and are designed to meet a specific objective. A Program may be ongoing (like SCORE counseling) or it may be time limited (like a 9-week accelerator program). A Program can be offered by one organization or by several. A Program's use does not depend on a specific physical place (even if it is conveniently hosted by one, it could be done somewhere else), The tools of a Program usually involve curricula, workbooks or binders, lectures, group discussions, and meetings.

Places are physical locations whose purpose is to house innovators and supply some of the physical needs unique to their ability to innovate. Co-working spaces and makerspaces are typical Places, although some large corporations may also have Places intended to foster innovation (Procter & Gamble, for example, has maintained a handful of off-site spaces for various innovation teams in Downtown Cincinnati over the past 10 years.) Places usually involve unusual or "creative" spaces, varieties of seating arrangements, white boards, and doors or dividers.

Nerve Centers are people or organizations that perform a traffic directing function: they help potential innovators or other participants find the right place to plug in among the variety of Programs and Places available. Nerve Centers do not own or control the larger system, but they are responsible for maintaining a comprehensive understanding of the larger system's offerings (such as Programs and Places), as well as its needs. Ideally, the Nerve Center will use its broader awareness to prod Programs and Places into addressing new challenges that the Nerve Center has encountered in its work. Nerve Centers may be designated as part of a system-building effort, or they may evolve into the role as the need for it arises.

Nerve Centers begin the process of transforming a collection of Places and Programs into a functioning system that can accelerate innovation beyond what an individual initiative can do. They create this opportunity by enabling participants to find the Programs and Pumps that best fit what they need - an often-overlooked function that can make the difference between a functioning system and a collection of tussling, half-fledged attempts.

Districts are physical places - ranging from a building to several city blocks - where physical design, economic activity, government involvement and culture are oriented to facilitating innovation. Districts may be master-planned or evolve organically, but they generally include

- A variety of Places and Programs intended to foster innovation,
- Spaces for businesses of varying sizes and growth,
- Public spaces and amenities designed to encourage interpersonal interaction, and
- Support activities such as restaurants, apartments and mailing services.

Coordination or collaboration among District elements may occur through some formal processes, but a District's implicit theory of how innovation will happen often relies on collisions and agglomeration effects as their primary methods. That is, they operate on the assumption that, by putting innovators in physical proximity and giving them places in which they can mix, innovation will occur organically as a result. We discussed in a previous chapter that the actual evidence to date throws a significant doubt on the actual effects of collision for fostering truly breakthrough innovation.

Issues of building and land use control, public policy objectives, public and private investment, private sector development and corporate support often play a significant role in how a District is initially formed and develops. Unlike other Pumps, Districts necessitate a relatively substantial real estate investment, both to house the District's activities and to demonstrate the kind of "buzz" needed to attract participants. This investment is often a mix of private and public funds and frequently results in some combination of adaptive reuse of existing buildings, new building construction, and physical infrastructure like sidewalks and transit stops.

Ecosystems are connected groups of all of the above elements. Many ecosystems are defined in terms of a geographic area, but those areas are larger than Districts and their identity is not typically tied to a physical place (it's not unusual for an Ecosystem to cover several counties). Ecosystems may focus on specific subsets of innovation, such as sustainable food production or biotech or disadvantaged entrepreneurs, but they may also be broadly defined.

Ecosystems rely heavily on their ability to communicate with and coordinate wide-flung collections of Programs and Places, and even Nerve Centers and Districts. They tend to function as a facilitator, coordinating participants and trying to align activities a broad range of activities in service of ecosystem - wide goals.

Obviously, all of these Pumps play important roles in the infrastructure. Programs increase the odds that an innovator knows how to keep herself afloat - most focus on business management and growth skills, which aren't many innovators' forte. And Programs give some entrepreneurs the hope that they're not insane to be trying this (despite the messages she may be getting from her grandmother or her neighbors).

Places give the innovator a physical connection to others pursuing the same ambitions, and he may find that he experiences a few lucky collisions while he parks his laptop at the table or waits to use the CNC machine.

In communities where the Innovation Infrastructure is starting to mature, Nerve Centers become crucial to helping the innovator land in the right place and get access to the right help quickly. Otherwise confusion and mixed messaging may lead the innovator to waste her limited time and money in the wrong place.

For work that benefits from close coordination, Districts can play a crucial role in easing an innovator's way, as we see how physical access and knowledge are still often knotted to each other. And Districts attract other innovators, drawn to the energy that a good district projects. Finally, Ecosystems place all of these within a larger context, facilitating for each innovator a reach and access that extends beyond any city block, making them part of a massive economic movement.

Most Innovation Infrastructures start with a Program, maybe a Place, and add a few more of these before the more complex structures take shape. Like physical infrastructure, innovation systems have a habit of evolving piecemeal, over time - someone notes a need, someone creates a new Pump. At first, that one Pump might do enough. But as the number of people increases and the complexity of their needs grows, those individual systems pretty quickly become overwhelmed, like when increased development forces houses that used artesian wells to hook up to a new water line.

But here's an important point: the household in that example I just gave had the ability to hook up to that water line because, maybe many years before, a team of planners thinking about how the area might change in the future anticipated that this area might need a water line. Based on that plan, the engineers calculated the amount of water it should carry and designed the system of pipes, valves, joints, pumps and more that would be required to deliver that water from its source to this house.

The water pipes didn't just appear there, and the Pumps don't often grow their own connections.

Someone envisioned and laid out what was needed for the whole system to work.

That's our big challenge. But before we get there, let's take a look at how the Pumps ultimately become able to do what we need them to -- by connecting to each other via the Pipes.

The Pipes

"Pipes" as we are using the term in our infrastructure analogy, are not so much *things,* like the organizations and buildings that we thought about when talking about the Pumps. The Pipes, instead, are the *types of interactions* that the Pumps may have with each other. The value – the importance – of the pipe in a water system isn't fundamentally in its width or depth or angle, unless those end up causing problems. The value of the pipe is in the degree of efficiency and effectiveness with which it can convey water to where it is needed.

By the same token, the value of the Pipes in our Innovation Infrastructure does not lie in whether the Pumps share information by meetings, agendas, web sites, Skype calls, or whatever, unless the methods being used create or exacerbate other problems.

Instead, the issue that defines what we need to know about our Pipes is: *How are the Pumps in our system relating to each other via the Pipes?*

In other words, how are the Pumps working together (or not working together)?

Every person who works with Innovation and entrepreneurship would probably fill in this chart a little differently. But an idealized set of Pipes in operation today might be classified like this:

	Program	Place	Nerve Center	District	Eco-system
Program	Collaborate	Host	Feed	Collide	Connect
	Compliment	Drive traffic	Filter	Recruit	Extend
Place	Host	Collaborate	Host	Catalyze	Example
	Drive traffic	Compliment	Embody	Focus	Node
Nerve Center	Feed	Host	Collaborate	Host	Respond
	Filter	Embody	Compliment	Embody	Adapt
District	Collide	Catalyze	Host	Collaborate	Anchor
	Recruit	Focus	Embody	Compliment	Distinguish
Eco-system	Connect	Example	Responsive	Anchor	Collaborate
	Extend	Node	Adapt	Distinguish	Compliment

A little explanation, since it's hard to communicate multi-dimension relationships in a two-dimensional format. The Pumps from the last chapter are listed across the top and down the side, so that each cell indicates how one Pump from the side and one from the top typically seem to interact with each other. Since the same five Pumps are listed both horizontally and vertically, most of the pairs of Pumps actually show up in two cells. Also, each kind of Pump has one cell where it is interacting with the same kind of Pump, since that does actually happen -- for example, there's a cell for how two Places interact.

In each cell, the two interactions listed may move one-way or two-way.

So that we have the same language moving forward, here is what I mean by each Pipe name:

Host: one Pump provides a physical space in which another Pump operates. Most Programs are hosted by a Place, like an innovation center in a university.

Collide: one Pump provides a context or stage in which members of other Pumps may find each other. A District's coffee houses or meetup events are often valued for their Collision potential.

Refer: one Pump directs a person to another Pump that has the tools that person needs, because the first Pump does not have them but knows that the second one does. One of a Nerve Center's primary functions is to know when a person should be referred to one Program over another.

Screen: similar to Referring, but in this case the Pump that first encounters the person actively evaluates whether the person is a good fit for a specific Program. When a Nerve Center or an Ecosystem determines that a product is far enough along in development to be referred to a high-growth accelerator, or it concludes that the founder needs a little more coaching to get to that point, then the Nerve Center or Ecosystem has screened the business on behalf of the Program.

Connect: Like any entrepreneurs, Innovation Infrastructure members live or die by being able to find the right help at the right time. An Ecosystem's high level point of view can help it connect a Program to another that has figured out how to solve a tough problem.

Inform: All Pumps need information about what is working, what is not, what new ideas they might try, and so on. Providing information on new regulations allows a District, for example, to help its Places avoid costly violations.

Embody: For the non-physical Pumps, like Ecosystems, being able to point to others who demonstrate the benefits of what they are trying to do can strengthen their case for support. Similarly, a Place or District trying to demonstrate its legitimacy may benefit from being associated with a Switchboard or Program that embodies a higher objective than simple profit.

Destination: A Place or a Program can provide a location within a District that both brings in new people and allows people to mentally anchor the more abstract organization to a specific spot on the map. This can be particularly important for building popular or funder support.

Node: a Node is a conduit to a group of people who can be of value to another Pump. When a Program asks a District to promote its event to its mailing list, the District is providing the Program with a Node that allows it to easily reach more people than it could by itself.

Respond: Pumps Respond to each other by answering questions, working together to solve issues raised by one of them, redesigning events to make them more useful to others, and so on. Responsiveness is arguably the hallmark of a healthy Innovation Infrastructure.

Strong Pipes and Weak Pipes

So that all sounds pretty productive, and we can start to see how the Pipes benefit the overall Infrastructure. But it often doesn't play out this way. But in terms of how these relationships actually develop, sometimes the Pipes don't work so well. This section gives a summary of common beneficial and less-beneficial ways in which the Pumps often connect to each other.

Here's a matrix similar to the last one:

	Program	Place	Nerve Center	District	Eco-system
Program	Compete	Window dressing	Exclude	Window dressing	Exclude
	Undercut	Minimize	Misunde-stand	Minimize	Misunder-stand
Place	Window dressing	Compete	Exclude	Window dressing	Exclude
	Minimize	Undercut	Misunder stand	Minimize	Overlook
Nerve Center	Exclude	Exclude	Compete	Ignore	Ignore
	Misunder-stand	Misunder stand	Undercut	Exclude	Exclude
District	Window dressing	Ignore	Ignore	Compete	Exclude
	Minimize	Exclude	Exclude	Undercut	Ignore
Eco-system	Exclude	Exclude	Ignore	Exclude	Compete
	Misunder-stand	Overlook	Exclude	ignore	Undercut

Let's unpack this in terms of the kinds of impact that ineffective Pipes can have on the Pumps:

Programs

A large number of Programs seem to view themselves as being in competition with other Programs that are in generally the same space, such as entrepreneurship education programs. It's often not an overt competition, since they are typically eager to present themselves as a "social good" type of program, but many will not hesitate to recruit a potential entrepreneur or funder who might objectively be more aligned with another program.

Many Programs are designed as non-profit corporations, and this model's constant fundraising pressure may exacerbate this competition. One way that Programs may deal with the conflict between being driven to compete and not wanting to appear to compete is by choosing to operate in isolation, running their own full set of programs in parallel to others.

Programs and Places often have something of a symbiotic relationship -- the Program benefits from a stable space, and the Place benefits from having something driving new attendees into their space. And Programs benefit from Nerve Centers that are able to direct good candidates to them (one advantage of having a Pipe to a Nerve Center is that the latter should be able to evaluate whether a new innovator is a good "fit" for the Program.) And of course the Nerve Center needs a good set of Programs to refer people to, since by definition they cannot take care of everyone themselves.

But if a Program concludes (accurately or not) that a Nerve Center or Place is treating them unfairly, or if a Nerve Center or Place concludes (accurately or not) that a Program cannot deliver on its promises, then the Pipe is broken and each is weaker.

Similarly, Programs are crucial to Districts and Ecosystems, since Programs teach the skills that the more complex organizations need and provide an easy-to access group of participants to populate the system. But again, a Program that is perceived to be failing to do what the larger system needs will be frozen out, possibly without an honest discussion of the concerns. And if a Program thinks that the District or Ecosystem is failing to support them (especially if they are hanging on by a thread, like many small nonprofits), resentment is likely to grow.

Places

At the present time, Places seem to have a higher mix of self-funded business models than do Programs. It appears to be more likely for a Place, such as a co-working facility or a makerspace, to gain the majority of its income from memberships and rentals, while few Programs can live solely off of their fees. This can have some benefits in terms of greater independence from foundations and the like, but it can also be risky, as the surprise closings of the TechShop makerspace network and the struggles of Regis demonstrated in 2016 and 2017.

Places can also compete with each other, but as long as they are competing in the private market for space, this competition does not seem to cause any damage to the Infrastructure. As Places proliferate in a market, however, their ability to complete appears to depend more and more on their ability to generate (and project) a Program- or District-like sense of community. Places may position themselves to appeal to a specific sector or demographic - one Place even differentiated itself by co-locating with a gym and appealing to people who wanted a health - centered community.

Obviously, connecting into a larger network should make it easier for a Place to recruit new residents -- and share the cost of events and promotions to attract them. As a result, Places may be eager to construct a Pipeline to a Nerve Center, a District or an Ecosystem, since any of these can be sources of referrals and partners for events, and their larger profile can lend legitimacy to a new or small Place. A Place can also benefit from being able to connect its members to other resources, such as conferences, webinars, technical support, etc. But if the Place is not perceived as adding value to the larger district, or the more publically-minded elements of the ecosystem view them as too mercenary, then this Pipe may also fail.

Nerve Center

Since a Nerve Center's value is inherently tied to its ability to connect the otherwise unconnected, the strength of a Nerve Center has a heavy correlation to the number of Pumps of all types that it can refer to, obtain hosting from, make suggestions to, etc. Conversely, the weakness of a Nerve Center stems from the degree to which other elements of the Infrastructure engage constructively, or ignore efforts to build stronger Pipes.

More than any other Pump (with the possible exception of the Ecosystem), the Nerve Center's success or failure depends on the amount of trust other participants are willing to put into it. When trust is strong, the Nerve Center can also have a legitimizing effect on the District or Place that hosts it. When this is not the case, however, the Switchboard may be the swiftest of the Pumps to be dismantled.

Districts

Districts represent a level of complexity several orders above the other Pumps. While Programs and Places and Switchboards are typically the work of one organization, Districts and Ecosystems are not so neatly owned: the official management may belong to one organization, but that entity is profoundly dependent on the other Pumps that fall within its boundaries. In a sense, a District or an Ecosystem can be defined by the agglomeration of other organizations that it contains, but when the system of Pipes is strong, a District's impact should exceed the sum of its parts.

A District, more than any of the other Pumps, depends on the impact of both physical space design and intentional systems for fostering a dense, thick web of human interaction. As we've discussed, a Program can use someone else's space, a Place at its minimum is a holder in which people do things, and a Nerve Center's basic functions could be run out of someone's house (most aren't).

A District, however, is known by both the quality of its buildings, streets, parks, transit stops, etc, and by the human energy that the spaces facilitate. A strong District not only hosts an array of Programs, Places, businesses and people, but both its physical design and its programs of activities are designed to help people to connect -to almost make it impossible for them not to connect. The term used for the kinds of serendipitous connections these places hope to engender is "collision," and we'll talk about that more in a future chapter.

Districts also have a sort of symbiotic relationship with Programs, Places and Switchboards: by hosting these Pumps in an interesting, dense, connection-rich environment, The District both gives the organizations access to more resources and lends them a certain cachet, since they can claim that they are in an Innovation District.

But the reputation of the District, especially over the long terms, relies on the success of the collection of other Pumps. If the parts are not themselves able to demonstrate the kinds of impacts that make funders and investors and political supporters happy, the District may have a hard time making the case for the kinds of physical investments it needs.

Some Districts, like many university research centers, are physically and functionally monolithic - many buildings are purpose-built for that specific type of innovation, and most people in those Districts have similar education and professional expertise. Districts that have grown up in older urban areas, on the other hand, may include a very broad mix of people - from stereotypical tech workers to tourists to the poor and people of color who lived in the area for decades. This mix gives these areas a vitality that many innovators seem to crave, but it also can mean that these Districts become places that have to confront and negotiate the complexity of how very different people live. This can raise some significant tensions, and they are not solved simply by planting street trees and installing bike lanes. We will explore these issues in an upcoming chapter.

Ecosystems

It should not be a surprise that Ecosystems include the most complex Pipe arrangements of all, since they may include a hundred Pumps and several hundred individual innovators. Ecosystems face the dual-edged challenge of being intensely needed by their participants, who know firsthand how much they depend on their connections, and being largely invisible to the general public.

Part of this invisibility is intentional - the Ecosystem wants to keep focus on successful businesses, not on itself. But, like a biologic ecosystem, innovation Ecosystems are also hard to perceive and understand because of their fuzzy boundaries. Ask a biologist to define what is inside and outside of the ecosystem of your local park, and you may get anything from microbes to birds stopping over twice a year during migration. The boundaries are, by their nature, porous. So an innovation Ecosystem will inherently have difficulty defining what it in it and what it without.

Because of its scope and its porousness, Ecosystems often seem to struggle to demonstrate their impact, and this is a key dimension of their Pipe connections. Optimally, the Ecosystem should be continually broadening the reach of every Pump within it. The Ecosystem should be the source of more information, more examples, more contacts, more potential partners, more new solutions and more opportunities than any other part of the ecosystem.

But even more than the District, which at least has solid physical resources to fall back on, the Ecosystem has to be able to demonstrate to its supporters that it is directly making it possible for the other Pumps to make a significant impact -- and be able to convert that impact into sustainable funding. This question of impact, and of measurable, significant, compelling impact, will become a key issue when we get to our final chapters.

"Operate in Isolation" and "Compete"

If you have been examining the matrix at the top of this section, you may have noticed that the words "Operate in Isolation" and "Compete" occur in each of the cells where one of the Pumps is interacting with another Pump of the same type. We discussed this specifically with regard to the Programs and Places, but not with the others. So why does that appear in each of these cells?

This is a bit of an artifact of the method -- Switchboards, Districts and Ecosystems are still rare enough and physically differentiated enough that they don't yet have to interact with each other very often. But I left these cells in there to highlight what I think is a significant risk -- one that we are seeing clearly among Programs and Places, and are likely to see among the others as they proliferate.

People who start Programs and Places, like any kind of entrepreneur or innovator, do it because they see an unmet need and a vision for how to fill it. While some kinds of business owners relish the adrenaline of competition and the fight to get the upper hand over the crowd, I don't think I've ever seen that drive in a

Program or Place founder (probably because you can have more success fighting for the spoils in other fields). Plus, people who see these kinds of Programs and Places as solutions are the ones who found that having a community was crucial to their own growth, so they don't seem naturally inclined to operate in isolation.

So why does this keep happening? Why do we keep encountering Programs and Places that resist opportunities to connect their Pipes to others -- insisting that their people/process/purpose is too unique to collaborate, avoiding sharing information with others, or simply not responding to invitations to share? Plenty of Programs and Places do collaborate, of course, but why do some turn down the Pipes extended from others?

There's probably as many specific reasons as founders, and we will touch on some particularly delicate possibilities in a future chapter. But one structural issue seems to exacerbate this problem - and this is why I left those words in not only the Programs and Places cells, but those of the Switchboards, Districts and Ecosystems as well:

They way we fund and operate the whole collection of Pumps leads us to treat them like disconnected parts -- like things that are supposed to operate in total isolation, that should only depend on themselves. As is so often true, we get what we pay for. The next chapter will unravel more of these unintended consequences.

How the Innovation Infrastructure Leaks

In traditional infrastructure construction, leakage occurs when the thing to be carried, like water through pipes, falls out along the way and does not make it to the intended destination. In traditional economics, "leakage" occurs when people buy goods and services outside of the local economy (such as when I buy a book from Amazon instead of the locally-owned bookstore).

In Innovation Infrastructure, **leakage occurs when then energy, creativity, and problem-solving capacity of the people who can innovate does not result in the innovations that it could have**. That might be because the innovators didn't have the right support, didn't have the appropriate information, couldn't access the skills, or didn't know what they didn't know (or have).

It's what happens when a promising business moves because they can't find the right talent, when a starry-eyed entrepreneur fails because she didn't understand the competition before investing all her savings, when one of the Pumps finds that it is not showing enough impact to keep its funders happy.

Arguably, some leakage is bound to happen -- even high-voltage electric wires leak a percentage of their power between the generator and the house. Even with the best information and collaborators, a seamless support network, great advisors, you name it, businesses can fail for reasons that no one can predict or control. Most people who have worked with innovators or entrepreneurs have seen that. It's treated as a truism.

But we have to be honest: in an awful lot of places, our Innovation Infrastructure leaks like a cheesecloth bucket. Despite hundreds of Pumps and Pipes across the US and Canada, despite millions of dollars invested in entrepreneurship and innovation fixes since the 1980s,

- The rate of new business starts continues to decline,[20]
- The rate of innovation, as proxied by patents, continues to decline,[21] and
- The rate of small businesses that survive their first five years (barber shop, tech startup, the numbers hold fairly steady across the board) hovers around 1 in 5. 20%.

Let's just take that last number for a minute. Give or take a few percentage points, the proportion of businesses of any type that survive their first five years is....

If it were a grade, we would have failed miserably. If it were a mortality rate for a part of our population, we would have an horrible national crisis. If it were

---

[20]https://money.cnn.com/2016/09/08/news/economy/us-startups-near-40-year-low/index.html
[21]https://www.brookings.edu/research/eleven-facts-about-innovation-and-patents/

number of houses at risk of demolition in a city, we would have an impending catastrophe.

And yet, we take this rate of failure among small businesses - the ones that we say are our economic future - as an inevitability, as a necessary cost of doing business. "Churn," we call it at the macro scale. "She made some mistakes and she couldn't recover," we shrug at the local level. "You can't learn unless you risk failing," we philosophize.

Meanwhile, the new economy grows glacially, income and wealth divides get worse, governments struggle to support basic services, the risks of being too dependent on old industries grow, and the Pumps that are supposed to power the new economy strain over and over to justify their meager existence.

Something's leaking. And no one seems to know where.

That lack of knowing where is partly a problem of good data. That 1 in 5 number that I quoted before? That's a national-scale metric that has become almost a rubric, in part because no one has any better. Are the entrepreneurs in that disadvantaged neighborhood doing better or worse than 1 in 5? Are more than 20% of our tech startups lasting to Year 5? Did that accelerator program bump those numbers upwards, or no?

In far too many cases, no one really knows.

We'll talk more about data in a minute. But keeping in mind that our available data can raise more questions than it answers, here are a few issues that we should examine as we try to figure out why we are leaking.

The Tech/Non-tech divide

Very few Pumps avoid making a distinction between "Tech" and "Non-tech." If you are preparing to open a bakery, your odds of getting into a Y Combinator-style accelerator are about nil, no matter what your scale potential looks like.

Tech-focused Pump managers will tell you that this is because tech founders are somehow different from Main Street-style entrepreneurs. Certainly there's a grain of truth to that - Main Street businesses need to deal with issues like inventory management, while they typical app builder doesn't. Meanwhile, tech startup people appreciate opportunities to discuss the latest Python extension or Github stack with people who also know what they are talking about, and chances are our bakery owner doesn't fit that definition.

But these boundaries aren't anywhere near as neat as this easy dichotomy seems to imply. And that creates two potential Leakages:

1) **Tech companies that need brick-and-mortar functions may not be able to get that help.** The largest recipient of venture capital (the usual golden standard for successful tech startup) in

Ohio in 2016 was a company called Everything But the House. EBTH conducts online estate auctions - you follow an item being auctioned through the web site, you place a bid if you want to buy, you get a notice if you get outbid, and you pay electronically before you pick the item up. Clearly, software, user interface and database design are crucial to this company's success - and they're good at it. But what else do they have to be able to do to be successful?

- Appraise an enormous array of items that range from art to children's clothes to industrial equipment
- Contract successfully with people who are parting with beloved possessions
- Rent and maintain warehouse space
- Manage hundreds of employees who sort and move items, verify payments, authorize release of items, deal with complaints, and more.

These aren't problems you can solve with a better stack management system or a larger server. To manage these elements of their business, EBTH needed some very traditional skills, both specialized (appraisal) and standard (warehouse management, negotiation, human resources). If a new company like this gets put in the "tech" bucket, where will they find help on warehouse management?

2) **Tech and "non-tech" innovators lose crucial opportunities to learn from each other.** EBTH

is just one large example of an often-overlooked truth: online sales requires substantial offline support. At the same time, traditional Main Street retailers frequently complain that their in-person sales are declining because it's easier (and often cheaper) for people to buy an item online. A large number of specialty retailers are supplementing their in-store sales with online, and downtown program managers tell me that they are seeing a small but growing number local retailers cut back on the amount of their store displaying goods for in-person customers - and devote more of their space to inventory storage and packaging/shipping. An increasing number of businesses are also giving up on the storefront entirely, choosing to make their living entirely online.

Obviously these two types of entrepreneurs could learn a lot from each other. Main Street retailers find their hands tied by the constraints of existing internet sales platforms (for example, Etsy products must be handmade or vintage), and tech entrepreneurs are trying to figure out how keep inventory in stock. Keeping these two separated deprives both of learning about the solutions that the others have discovered.

This Leakage isn't just important to retailers; it's an indicator of a larger problem with the tech-nontech division, and indeed with many of the arbitrary barriers that we have put up:

Diversity of thought and experience is absolutely crucial to uncovering new solutions. If we are stuck inside the limits of our own experience, we miss the potential solutions that we just have not yet encountered.

The scaling vs. "Lifestyle" divide

Another common barrier falls between businesses that are determined to be "scaleable" - a loosely-defined term that generally means "might make enough revenue to attract a large sum of money from an investor" -- and those that are "lifestyle" operations. "Lifestyle" businesses employ the owner and others -- perhaps one associate, perhaps a couple of hundred, as in a locally-owned restaurant with two or three locations. Lifestyle businesses are not looking for eight-digit investments, or to be in everyone's home in North America, or to be the next Facebook. But they are intending to be in business, generating income, paying taxes, and perhaps employing people, for years or decades to come.

Economic developers, university tech transfer offices and public officials largely created this Leakage years ago when they decided that public investments would go into businesses that would generate as many jobs (and as much positive press) as when they recruited a business to move to town. So just as economic development incentives were offered to new businesses, but not to existing businesses maintaining their operations, the lion's share of public investment was designated for "scale-able" businesses. Again, planning to open a bakery and employ a hundred in a few years? Even if you've got a new technology for cooking (but you're not interested in selling that tech worldwide), your local program for scale-able startups may have some funds... but they're probably not for you.

As before, this Leakage has at least two unwanted side-effects:

1) Since we're not very good at picking winners and losers, **we tend to waste a good deal of the support we have to offer**. Remember that one-in-five number for new business failures? There is no evidence to indicate that this is different for businesses designated as "scaleable," and a good deal to indicate that it's roughly the same. While those optimistic bets placed on the scaleable-designated sometimes pay off, they very often don't (hence, the high-risk, high-return mechanics of venture capital). And even when they do, they may not bring the benefits we were hoping for, as we'll explore at the beginning of Part 3.

2) Focusing our attention on the businesses that we have decreed "scaleable" discounts the crucial value that all the rest of our new businesses have the potential to have -- not only in terms of creating innovative solutions,

but in terms of the basic bedrock of economically-healthy communities: sustainable, decent-paying jobs, keeping money in the community, and opportunities to build wealth (especially for those who have been cut off from those opportunities for generations).

The loss of locally-owned, stable businesses has been consistently identified as a core underpinning of a host of urban and rural challenges, from lack of positive role models to retail leakage to building deterioration to crumbling tax base.

It's like growing a field of peppers, but focusing all our fertilizer and pest removal on the one plant with the prettiest blossoms, while the others grow blighted and get worms. Pragmatically, we'd probably make more money off of a field full of decent peppers than off three prize specimens and a pile of buggy third-rate vegetables. But one can argue that this is exactly what we do when we decide that "scale-able" businesses are more important than others.

Intrapreneurs and entrepreneurs. Most people in the general public know what it is to be an entrepreneur, and they have at least a sense of what it means to innovate. But what's an intrapreneur? My answer: a resource that we don't support, and don't benefit from, often enough.

An intrapreneur is responsible for innovation inside a large organization. The intrapreneur is trying to create a new product, or reposition a brand to fit an emerging market, or design a more efficient internal system using new technologies. They might work with a team, or they might be alone. They might have formal training in innovation thinking or econometric modelling or materials research, or they might just have a hunch that there's a better way to do it. They might be fully supported by the company, designated as an Intrapreneur, or they might be just trying to innovate under the radar. And, because larger corporations are complex and people aren't always rational, they might be more than one of these at the same time.

One can argue that intrapreneurship is easler than entrepreneurship (every entrepreneur longs occasionally for a stable paycheck), but I think successful intrapreneurship is a lot harder. When you are an intrapreneur,[22] you are not only pushing against the barriers that most start-ups face (not enough money/staff/time, hard to explain what you're doing, people tell you it won't work), but you are also doing so from *inside an organization that is designed to protect itself from risks.*

---

[22] Full disclosure: I was an intrapreneur for three years within a large engineering company. Also, my husband has a similar (but better supported and more successful) role in the company he works for today.

Corporate sign-off policies, expense reporting mandates, hierarchy reviews, budgeting processes and more are designed to protect the company from taking any action that could cut into its profits or open it up for liability. As most intrapreneurs can tell you, fighting your way through the approval process is one of the most challenging and least rewarding parts of the job. And it's one that can expose the intrapreneur to a lot of personal risk -- unless the company has a very strong intrapreneurship support culture, it's not difficult for an intrapreneur to find herself on the street after a change in leadership or an economic crisis. Very few companies have that kind of intrapreneurship support.

Pumps, especially those that focus on technology and scalable startups, often lean into courting their local corporations. And corporations are frequently eager to get involved in the innovation scene, because it's often easier for them to acquire or partner with a smaller company that has developed an innovation than to try to get it birthed through their own systems.

But corporate involvement often seems to stay at arms-length: the big business may sponsor events, or put their name on the front entrance wall, or do a matchmaking session with entrepreneurs, and they may even end up contracting a startup to develop a concept product -- or recruit a new intrapreneur. But they find almost no opportunities to play a direct role in the innovation ecosystem.

Like the other somewhat-arbitrary barriers, this one results in at least two Leakages:

1. Intrapreneurship is even less studied that entrepreneurship, but evidence appears to indicate that *most intrapreneurs are isolated, both from others who are trying to operate within the company and from innovators outside the company.* With the exception of few programs that are so rare that they show up in business textbooks (Procter & Gamble's Connect+Develop being a well-used example), most intrapreneurs lack the kind of innovation-focused, forward-looking environment that most Pumps of any type create. Some newer opportunities, such as the Innov8tors conferences held in cities worldwide, can overcome some of that isolation but many intrapreneurs may not have the company support to participate in events like that.

   Since intrapreneurship and innovation are crucial to the long-term health of the companies that are often our biggest employers and tax payers, allowing their intrapreneurs to flounder is not in our larger self-interest. If an intrapreneur can find a network of support within the larger Innovation Infrastructure, that will increase the odds that the intrapreneur is able to provide the value that the company (and we) need her to provide.

2. Corporations, as we have noted before, run on internal processes that are designed to protect the company from risks, a strategy that bleeds over into the conventional company/contractor relationship that typically allows an entrepreneur to work with an intrapreneur and his company. But finding entrepreneurs who are a good fit for working with the larger corporation is not as simple as reviewing a website and a LinkedIn page.

Fear of risk, of being sold false goods, of signing a contract with someone who "won't work with us" puts a significant level of braking -- and a lot of legal review -- on the intrapreneur who sees an opportunity to work with an outside innovator. And yet, the distance that is maintained between many Pumps and their potential corporate partners makes it difficult for intrapreneurs to develop the kind of deep knowledge and trust relationship that would strengthen the intrapreneur to fight the system for the contract's approval. Enabling the intrapreneur to truly and intentionally mix with the rest of the innovation community[23] could unlock new synergies and new opportunities that neither the intrapreneur nor the entrepreneur realize until they get to know each other.

---

[23] The intrapreneur has to protect the company's confidential information and intellectual property and all that, of course, but the average intrapreneur has to do that when she goes home for dinner anyways.

Elitism

Most Innovation Infrastructure members don't think of themselves as elitist or exclusionary. Most Pumps make a point of saying that they are open to everyone, and more and more are actively trying to recruit more diverse membership (especially the ones that had had a tech focus, since that industry has received so much bad press for hiring predominantly white and male). But claiming inclusivity and truly living it are often not the same thing.

Any Pump can undercut its claim of inclusivity through a variety of seemingly mundane details. A Place that lacks closed-off conference rooms with decent soundproofing can make life miserable for a team that comes from a culture where people argue animatedly. A Program that relies on retired executives to coach entrepreneurs from disadvantaged communities may find that the experience causes more confusion for its participants than it helps. An Ecosystem that claims to include everyone but hosts a conference where only one panel member is from a minority population sets itself up to be viewed with skepticism. And a District whose board of directors consists of 10 white men and one Asian woman may be projecting a very clear message about who is and who is not welcome here.

For many people, these kinds of insensitivities have an ethical component - they should not happen because they are not a good way to behave in the 21st century. But these kinds of inadvertent elitism also create very practical, very damaging Leakages:

1. One of the common complaints laid against startups is that some companies spend *hundreds of hours and thousands of dollars to build things that are only useful to a small population* - often one that looks a lot like themselves. For years, I have been a volunteer coach for an entrepreneurship "pitch" event at a large university. Every year, I end up reviewing 20 or 30 business concepts... and every year more than half of them are directly aimed at the narrow market of college students facing some specific challenge that they encountered earlier in the school year.

   I don't blame these student teams for designing a solution to their own needs -- that's a hallmark piece of advice for entrepreneurs.[24] The problem is that they don't have a wide enough view of the world to empathize with, and thus perhaps identify innovations for, people who don't look or sound like they do.

   Early on in this book I noted that one of our learnings from Econogy was that *diverse teams find better solutions.* An innovator who only knows people who look and sound like her will

---

[24] (and aspiring young writers, who get told over and over again to quit trying to tell lurid stories of bullfights a la Hemingway and write about what you know).

limit her pursuit of a worthwhile challenge to solve - she will limit it to the problems that face people who look and sound like her. If she had a wider understanding of the world, and if she had the opportunity to co-create with people who come from a different background, she might find her eyes open to a much more valuable (and profitable) opportunity.

So when we inadvertently limit our Innovation Infrastructure to a narrow range of innovators, we effectively deprive them of some of the tools that they need to do innovations that are worth doing.

2. People who have been systematically or routinely excluded, overlooked or disrespected may be unlikely to tell you to your face-- especially if they feel that they need your help or acceptance or they don't know whether you will take criticism well. So in many cases, the leaders of the organization that has inadvertently excluded people may never know what impact they have had. *But the people who have been on the receiving end of that experience seldom truly forget* - and the trust needed for collaboration is broken, again denying the larger innovation community of the benefits of rich diversity. Restoring trust in the diverse innovation community, just like in any relationship, requires a long-term dedication to transparency, honesty, and determined effort to improve.

Data, data, data

In *Beyond Collisions,* Maria Meyers of Kansas City's SourceLink does an excellent job of demonstrating the value of a story in terms of generating support for what we have termed an Innovation Ecosystem. As Maria notes, a story of a successful entrepreneur makes the benefits of a relatively abstract and invisible program come to life - the funder knows that his money not only does this thing, but that it makes a direct impact on people like the one highlighted.

She's right. Stories are powerful. But from my perspective, many Pumps rely far too heavily on feel-good stories, and invest far too little in something that we tell new businesses all the time to do:

Identify your measures of success, measure whether you are achieving them, evaluate, adjust, and do it over and over again, as quickly as you can.

Most Programs can tell you how many people went through a class, and maybe they have a feedback survey from graduation day. Most Switchboards can tell you how many referrals they made last year. Most Ecosystems can tell you the amount of money that their participants invested, and some Districts even have impressive-looking Impact Reports that estimate millions of dollars in primary and secondary economic activity resulting from their businesses. But what do they not answer?

- What percentage of the area's total potential (or actual) entrepreneurs are we serving?
- How are the ones we worked with doing compared to the others?
- How many of our participants have a stable, sustainable business five years later?
- Who is filling the new jobs? Are they people who have lived here who are moving up to better jobs, or are we attracting people from somewhere else?

There's reasons, of course, why we don't have answers to these questions. The data isn't easy to get, and some that is might be out of date. We haven't been doing it long enough to have long-term results yet. The businesses don't want to answer those questions, or just don't want us to bother them.

And in a lot of cases, it may be more comfortable, more convenient, less nerve-wracking to focus on those happy stories and a few promising pinpoints rather than to take a critical look at our cherished efforts. It takes a rather brave person to stand in the 360-degree mirror, and most of us don't want to see all our flaws in that harsh light.

But there's some significant Leakages that come from this lack of data:

1. We end up making *decisions based on assumptions, hunches or guesses, instead of factual information.* This means (and has meant) that we can put a lot of money and time and energy into something that isn't having the impact we really need (we may know that it's not having that effect, or we may not).

2. Our *funders and supporters grow suspicious* of our rosy claims and start asking for answers that we do not have.

3. Our funders and supporters may say nothing at all, but they may conclude from the limited information that they can get that we are not making the promised impact, and they may quietly shift their priorities to something else.

As we've said more than once, we are at a moment in history where we face massive challenges that we need to solve, fast. We need new technologies, but we also need **new ways of working, new ways of managing information, new ways of collaborating, and much more.**

We cannot avoid a small measure of inefficiency in our Innovation Infrastructure - as lean startup acolytes and poets alike know, creativity requires mistakes, missed turns, failures and pivots. An acceptance of less-than-perfect results has spread over to Innovation Ecosystems from that experience.

But our Innovation Infrastructure isn't working like a lean startup. We are missing large elements of what makes a Lean Startup strategy work.

We aren't looking critically at what we have built. We aren't examining the factual data that would indicate whether we are making a demonstrable impact. We aren't challenging our implicit biases, seeing and overcoming our own blinders, pulling people with different experiences from us into the process. We aren't asking ourselves whether the Pumps and Pipes we have built are actually doing the things that our world needs today.

We aren't learning and growing, nowhere near enough.

We're doing exactly what we tell entrepreneurs and innovators not to do. We are, far too often, acting more like Blockbuster and Kodak than like the success stories we tell our innovators to emulate.

And this is a worse flaw in us than it is in a business. If we are the managers of the Innovation Infrastructure, we responsible for not just our organization, but for the entire system on which those innovation-makers are depending. A civil engineer takes her job very seriously, because a mistake could have a direct and potentially catastrophic effect on hundreds of people.

We are responsible for the infrastructure that will enable the new economy. We are responsible for the places and systems that we all need to launch and accelerate the new economy that we need.

That's an enormous responsibility, and one that we sometimes seem to take too lightly.

Part 3 will help up reframe our work. We will turn our attention to how we can create a fully effective Innovation Infrastructure -- one that accelerates all of us into the new economy and the new universe of solutions awaiting us.

Part III. Innovation Infrastructure for the New Economy

The last two Parts of this book have examined how we have built and managed our Innovation Infrastructure so far, and how what we have built is failing to live up to the high challenges that we need it to address. In this Part, we will unpack a detailed vision for how we can redesign our Innovation Infrastructure to play the role we need it to:

Catapult our cities, our cultures, our people and our world into the new economic age we are entering, and equip us all to thrive.

We do not have the luxury of settling for anything less.

In this Part, we will be focusing in on one of the Pumps: the Innovation District. That's not because Innovation Districts are any more important than any other Pump. But doing so at this time gives us some advantages:

- Innovation Districts are the most concrete of the two more complex Pumps (Innovation Districts and Ecosystems), and that will allow us to envision this approach in the most clear terms.

- Innovation Districts have a stronger inherent ability to attract funding and political/corporate support because they involve physical spaces. That creates some obvious benefits, but it also creates some deep challenges, since the stakes and the scrutiny are likely to be higher. As a result, it could be harder for an Innovation

District to shift to a new model if it starts out on the wrong tack, because existing investors with substantial stakes in the old approach may resist.

- Innovation Districts provide us with the best ability to envision the potential benefits of the new approach, since most of the ones we can call to mind exist in diverse urban areas where we can most easily encounter a broad mix of people, businesses and organizations.

But all of the following points will apply to you in some manner if your primary focus is a Place, a Program or anything else. It *is* an ecosystem, after all.

From here out, we're going to refer to Future-Ready Innovation Districts. That phrase captures a few key points:

- As I noted before, we don't have a universal name for this new era yet, so this term allows me to wiggle out of picking a phrase that might look silly in five years.

- Because this era is still emerging, and because we don't yet know exactly what it will require, this term reflects the same stance that the World Economic Fund took in outlining the 2020 skills that we talked about in Part 1: building the skills necessary to adapt to and manage in a complex and unpredictable world.

As we will note, innovators and entrepreneurs urgently need to be equipped with the skills that the WEF identified. And we will argue that one of the most crucial responsibilities of the Future-Ready Innovation District is to get them equipped.

- As we discussed at the end of Part II, too many elements of today's Innovation Infrastructure are acting more like old-school institutions than like the nimble, lean startup businesses we tell our participants to emulate. And an Innovation District, thanks to its physical footprint and all that comes with that, faces ever more barriers to nimble-ness than a Program or an Ecosystem. So embedded in this term is a core concept: a Future-Ready Innovation District has to consciously maintain the same foresight and ability to change that we expect of the businesses within it.

Again, keep in mind that everything that we say about a Future-Ready Innovation District applies in its own way to the other Pumps in the Innovation Infrastructure. Programs have to not only teach basic skills, but help participants understand the risks and opportunities that the emerging economy could offer. Nerve Centers have to be acutely aware of whether people in the system are being prepared for new opportunities, or only continuations of the old. Ecosystems must push their participants to look beyond their local horizons, and Places need to realize that their ability to thrive long term does not depend on providing funky new features (Foosball!! Indoor slide!!! [25]), but on their ability to increase their members' ability to become Future Ready themselves.

---

[25] As I write, there is a new co working space in Cincinnati whose social media advertising focuses on its price and the fact that it has an indoor slide. Like on a playground. Seriously.

The Future-Ready Innovation District, Described.

The next few chapters brings me back to that old challenge: describing an interrelated, complex tangle of interacting things in an uber-linear format. To do that, I'm going to go back to my roots in journalism: I'll break it down into the Who, What, Where, When, Why and How.

Given that we are focusing on Future Ready Innovation Districts, which we selected because of their physical concrete-ness, it might make sense to start with What or Where. And since we are talking about a new approach, some might think we should start with Why.

But I'm going to start with Who, not just because that's the way we learned the list in elementary school. Putting Who at the center of this description is necessary for several reasons:

- In the emerging economy, **Who is more at the center than ever before**. Innovation is a function of human creativity -- not capital, not real estate, not street trees, not granting programs. Whether we succeed or fail in this era will depend more than ever in human history on whether people can invent solutions, solve problems, and invent the things that we don't know yet that we need.

- **Who often gets overlooked**, especially in the more complex Pumps and Pipes, because we still have this Industrial-era wiring that tells us that the Organization drives progress. We invoke the Who, assert that we are serving the Who, write our grant applications around how we will impact the Who. And sometimes Programs and Places do manage to focus on Who, but too often they focus on individual Whos in an individual moment, without looking to the larger emerging trends and how to build a powerful engine of Whos to capitalize on those emerging trends.

- Just like Lean Startup and Design Thinking and a host of other new business strategies taught us, **Who is the elements of our Pump where we will learn the most**. Who, and especially Who as a diverse and inclusive whole, may see what we cannot. Of course, sometimes Who can be stuck in the present or the past, trying to cling to something familiar or unreflectively applying an out of date rule they internalized years ago (that's where the channeling I'll describe under What comes in).

Who?

Who has a very short answer: everybody. At least, everybody who can innovate. That means:

- Young people
- Old people
- People of color
- White people
- People who are poor
- People who are wealthy
- People who are female
- People who are male
- People who are not neurotypical
- People who are neurotypical
- People who have high level technical skills
- People who have "street" skills
- People who didn't finish high school
- People who have PhDs
- People who work for themselves
- People who work for Fortune 100 companies
- People who want to work on something Big
- People who want to work on something Small
- People who are fully inside the community
- People who participate occasionally
- People who know what they are trying to achieve
- People who are still looking for the thing they should achieve.

- People who are passionate about something.
- People who want to grow, learn, succeed.
- People who want to do something that matters.

If you can think of some more, add them.

As we discussed in Part II, almost no existing Pump fully lives up to this. Some may involve people whose skin comes in a wide variety of colors, but they are all "tech" people or "scale" people or "microenterprise" people. Some may say that they welcome everyone, but their traditional after-class trip to a loud bar excludes the person on the autism spectrum or the working mother who can't afford a $10 drink. Some claim to include everyone, but they effectively bar the doors to the intrapreneur who needs to know he's not nuts in order to have the impact that he has the unique ability to create.

In most cases, we're falling short on Who because

- Our "mission" has been to serve one or another subset (that is, our Industrial-Era wiring tells us that we have to stick to our lane, even if that fails to work in the emerging era).

- Our "mission" has been to serve those who are disadvantaged and thus can't play on the same field (read: our Industrial-Era wiring tells us that the historically disadvantaged need "help" and don't have valuable insights that the rest of us need in our routine innovative lives).

- We have never spent time with a certain population segment, and thus we didn't know how they could improve everyone else's insight.

Psychologists have identified three core types of diversity:

- Origin (your skin color, hair color, height, etc.)
- Experience (your life history, what you have experienced)
- Cognitive (how you tend to think and perceive the world)

If finding the solutions that we need requires new ways of thinking and solving, and if diverse groups are more likely to find creative solutions than unilateral groups, then it makes sense that a Future-Ready Innovation District will include the absolute most diverse range of people it can get.

Having said this, though, don't read it as an endorsement of the "Collision" theory of innovation. We talked about this previously, but to recap: Just because you put diverse people in the same physical place does not mean that they will interact.

Our deep-rooted tendencies to tribalism mean that we are far less likely of our own volution to seek out an interaction with someone who looks, sounds or acts different from ourselves, and we're more likely to regard them from the start with fear or suspicion. "Collisions" might happen occasionally, but they are far more likely to happen among two very similar people than among people who are significantly different. The idea that setting a stage conducive to collision will make innovation happen is a bit of magical thinking, especially if the type of innovation we are seeking is more than another widget of marginal value.

So the great challenge that a fully diverse Who creates is one of enabling that Who to fully unlock their potential. For this, we will turn to What.

What?

"Entrepreneurs are like cockroaches. We need to lay out the rich food for them and then get out of their way."
> -me, quoting a community development manager, speaking to economic development agencies in the central US, ca. 2012.

"Scratch a planner, find a dictator underneath."
> -me, quoting my economics professor, almost once a month 2001 - 2018

Nothing like having a documented personal history to make you laugh at yourself.

When we talk about What our Future Ready Innovation Districts should be doing, it's very easy for us to fall into one of these two extremes. We often take a hands-off, magical thinking approach -- if we just turn them lose on a pile of stuff they need, All the Good Things Will Happen. And we try not to notice when they don't.

Conversely, given the high stakes I've pointed to in this book, it might be tempting to create the World's Biggest Master Plan for our Future Ready Innovation District -- not just buildings and green spaces and Places, but the caliper of the trees and an exhaustive regimen of events, standards, certifications, expectations and more. Preferably all scribed in a hardbound, suitable-for-coffee-table book.

As we said in Part 1, one of the things that seems to characterize the emerging era is that binary and/or choices work more poorly than ever. We do not seem to be inclined as humans to sit easily with middle ways, but that is what we have to do.

Borrowing from an earlier book in which I dealt with a similar dichotomy regarding how urban planners interact with the public, I'm going to propose a middle way. I call it **channeling**.

Picture a small river in your mind. The river runs through a flat plain, and its banks are shallow. When water levels are low, the river runs through its accustomed space, and it runs at a consistent speed and volume. When it runs through the town, it may power a turbine in a dam, which uses the kinetic force of the water to create clean energy that allows other people to do productive things.

But when it rains hard, or the snow melts near its headwaters, the river quickly overflows its banks and floods the plaIn for several yards to either side. If you think of the water in terms of the potential energy that it carries, its ability to power the turbine, you will see that the water that now sits in the field does not carry much of that kind of energy. Except for a slow subsiding into the ground or back into the creek, the water demonstrates very little energy.

Of course, the water might have demonstrated a lot of energy when the river first rose, especially if there was a downpour or a beaver dam gave way upriver. If that happened, there was a short period where the water that overflowed the banks was very powerful – but not in a way that generated benefits. Perhaps the torrent uprooted some trees, or washed out a rabbit burrow. Since it's a natural ecosystem, there might be secondary benefits, like bare ground for new seeds to take root, but the water itself was not able to use its power to create any benefits.

Channeling, as we are using the term, is about guiding the motive force we are valuing (our Who) into making the best possible use of its energy for the benefit of themselves and the rest of the world. We shape the context in which we invite them to work such that it makes it easier for them to move in the direction that will produce the most value. We do not prevent them from overflowing the banks, but we smooth the path to help them achieve the biggest potential impact.

How do we create this Channel? These three components provide the foundation of that Channel. Different Future Ready Innovation Districts will build them out differently, depending on their unique Who and the rest of their context, but here are the fundamental components of the Channel:

1. **Facilitate Future Readiness.** If we need our innovators to help us all successfully move into this emerging economy, and if we know that most people to date have a fuzzy, at best,

understanding of what this might entail, then it's crucial that we equip innovators with the best available understanding of what this future looks like and what it will demand of them, regardless of what they are trying to achieve. Here's just a sampling of things that anyone trying to succeed needs, whether they're working on artificial intelligence or landscape management:

- how to **collaborate** with a diverse team.
- how to look for and adapt to the early **signs of change** in a given industry.
- how to build **collaborative networks** to supplement your skills.
- how to spot and unpack your own **biases**
- how to think from **first principles** to avoid unexamined assumptions..

Of course, teaching Future-Ready skills using Industrial Age teaching methods (lectures, desks, even Powerpoint dependence) would make no sense. These are not the kinds of insights that we can gain through rote memorization. Instead, Future-Ready skills have to be internalized, assimilated. How do we do that?

- Build the skills acquisition process around **practicing** these skills and insights immediately after being introduced to them

- Build Future-Ready language and skills into **every activity**, from casual dinners to formal public events.
- **Reinforce** this paradigm shift through daily opportunities to explicitly practice Future-Ready skills into the support that the Innovation District provides for each innovator (for example, through the Think Tanks described in the next section).

Will an innovator be willing to spend her precious time on building Future Ready skills? Especially if the client's web site is overdue, or she was up way too late finishing it last night, or she's got to get the pitch deck done for that presentation next week?

Maybe. Maybe not. The point of the Channel is to support the innovator in moving toward the goal as smoothly as possible. And support doesn't mean demanding attendance like a 19th-century schoolmarm. The point of the Future-Ready learning part of the Channel is to enable the innovator to internalize a Future-Ready Approach. If those resources are not just in a classroom, but are embedded throughout the Future Ready Innovation District, whether one attends a class or not isn't the determination of success.

2. **Accelerate Innovation through Intentional Diverse Colliding.** Most business start-up

approaches emphasize the need to get lots and lots of potential consumer feedback, but innovators consistently, seemingly universally, struggle to do that (fear of rejection, fear of being told that their idea won't work, fear of strangers? All of the above). And if we see now that diversity of feedback will increase the odds of finding a truly valuable solution, this challenge becomes even more acute.

As a result, the Channel function of our Future Ready Innovation District has to overcome this resistance and make it easier for our innovators to understand how diverse audiences interact with their innovation.

As we noted before, collisions *au naturel* are relatively unlikely to occur among the diverse members of a Future Ready Innovation District, and by expanding our definition of Who is included, we have only made that harder. But since what brings all of these people into the Innovation District is those last three points on the list -- a desire to learn, to grow, and to make a difference -- we can Channel participants into diverse, productive collaboration by making it easy for innovators to use that diversity to make their solutions more effective.

Here's a few specific ways we can build that part of the Channel:

- **Challenges**. Challenges can increase understanding of a Future Ready skill or issue by placing a focus on it and allowing participants to envision how their skills or product can address it. Since , given a meaty challenge, most participants are unlikely to feel that they have all the answers in themselves, this should encourage them to intentionally seek out people with complimentary dimensions of diversity. Crafting the Challenge will be key to this - it has to be relevant enough to merit attention, difficult enough to necessitate a highly diverse team, and yet concrete enough that a practical solution could be developed. Challenges could also be very useful in helping participants who have not yet identified their mission.

- **FutureReady Think Tanks.** An organization called the Ghana Think Tank helps people across the developed world create new solutions by connecting them to groups of innovators in developing countries, such as Ghana and Morocco. The Think Tank members bring their practical experience of innovating outside of the dominant culture to identify and develop ways to solve problems that the sponsor organization might have never encountered otherwise.[26]

FutureReady Think Tanks would provide a similar opportunity to tap the insight of people that the innovator might not encounter otherwise – while also raising the profile and validating the legitimacy of what others know. A Future Ready Think Tank can be assembled of people from inside or outside the Innovation District, but participants should be intentionally selected to provide the highest possible diversity along all dimensions. Think Tank members then have the responsibility to ask questions, challenge assumptions, make recommendations, propose alterations etc.

In most cases, Think Tank members should be paid for their advice as an additional means of validating the importance of their perspective, although the details may vary.

3. Create a **pattern of converging and diverging** to maximize all participants' ability to benefit fully. Converging and diverging design processes are commonly used in a wide variety of

---

[26]www.ghanathinktank.org/

business settings, and typically refer to a rhythm where a team of designers works independently for a period of time and then converge with other designers to get feedback, select sketches for future development, etc.

In a Future Ready Innovation District, converging and diverging will be crucial for two reasons. One is similar to the design use: Since participants are getting input from a much wider range of sources than usual, they will need time and space to integrate what they are hearing and decide what to incorporate and what to discard.

Perhaps more significantly, opportunities to diverge will be particularly important to people who need to reconnect in security with others who share their background. That might be people with similar technical skills ("Do you think we could actually build a component that does what the Think Tank member said?"), or it might be people who share a certain disadvantaged background (I think he's assuming I can't do it because I'm female. What should I do?")

People who are coming from diverse backgrounds are historically the ones who have felt excluded or unwelcome in many Innovation Districts, so we should expect that they will encounter unique challenges, even within an environment that values diversity. These people may need opportunities to connect with others of a similar background, both for solidarity and for peer advising. It's important that the Future Ready Innovation District not insist on some false "color-blindness" or fail to recognize that such "safe spaces" may be necessary.

Where?

It might be tempting for an urban planner like myself to use this opportunity to obsess over the latest urban design and transportation trends and turn this into a discussion of passive energy buildings, multi-modal transit, green stormwater retention and the like. But here's the interesting thing: Innovation Districts are already developing in a whole range of physical spaces: purpose-built and adapted, sleek and scruffy, concentrated and spread-out, auto-dependent and bike-friendly. An Innovation District doesn't have to look like an idealized Brooklyn, or a translucent futuristic city, or anything in particular (which is why we started with Who).

Physical design can feel like a good place to place your attention because, while it might be complicated, it's not complex. If you build a building, it stays put. If you plant a street tree, it grows there, not three blocks over. If you paint the walls pink because that's supposed to be calming, chances are it will stay reasonably pink. And investors like to see their name on a good-looking building, because it gives confidence that they have put their money into something that lasts. That's an important consideration, and one we'll discuss more in the section on How.

Whether it's rehabbed or purpose-built, though, there's a few key components of an Future Ready Innovation District's Where that warrant particular attention:

- **Design for flexibility.** Whether it's moveable walls, conduit space for future technology, furniture that can convert from shelf to conference table, or outdoor plaza sun screens that double as whiteboards, the role of the Future Ready Innovation District's spaces is to foster innovation, not block it. It's important not to overwhelm a space with too many alternative uses (a garden/conference room/kitchen/ poetry slam?), but think function options over pure form.

  The fact of the matter is that at this point in history, we don't know a lot about what the future of work, innovation and entrepreneurship will entail. Just in the past few years, we have largely eliminated the need for internet cables, HDMI cords, desktop monitors, storage space for binders and books, and many other elements that were necessary even in the early internet stages of business. Some features, like wet labs or commercial kitchens, require equipment and plumbing that needs to be installed in a fairly permanent manner, but how do we anticipate the businesses, coordination practices, technology, etc. that we will need to accommodate within our district in ten or 15 years?

- **Value of small spaces.** In the early days of the Downtown Project in Las Vegas, an accelerator member told me that their team had barely the amount of room they needed to work, and that was on purpose. The tight space channeled them to avoid anything superfluous and to share resources with other teams. Small spaces can create a sense of intimacy, of shared purpose and interests that can get lost in an expansive or isolated space. And it helps to overcome the Lonely Genius mindset that can hog-tie some stressed and frantic innovators who assume that they have to have all the answers within themselves.

- **Private options.** The value of small spaces, however, fades fast when someone can't concentrate due to the noise or distractions. And for some people, such as those who are sensitive to loud noises or lights, private options may make the difference between being able to participate or being rendered immobile.

  Most accelerators and co-working spaces and the like provide huddle rooms and little closets for private phone calls, but these are hardly spaces designed for deep thought. Many innovators would probably benefit from a convenient space that allows them to step away from the intense interpersonal world for some private thinking. A walking trail, a meditation space, even no more than a designated quiet room could provide a great benefit, especially for innovators who are introverted or, like many who experience Asperger's syndrome, find constant interpersonal interaction stressful and exhausting.

- **Quiet spaces.** Innovation-oriented spaces can feel like a beehive, and that's part of the intent of the open spaces and connectivity. But just like some innovators may need a respite from the public space, others may particularly benefit from places where they experience silence. As we discussed in Part 1, Future Ready Innovation that tackles the challenges that are worth tackling requires us to learn to think, to integrate information, to create new solutions. And while diverse teams are a crucial source of input, at some point any innovator probably needs some concentrated, uninterrupted thinking time to make sense of the inputs and discover that new solution.

  In the intensive world of interaction that a Future Ready Innovation District creates, finding the mental space to think can present a big challenge. Quiet meditation also seems to help our mental and physical health, too, which should be concerns of any Innovation District.

  Quiet spaces can hold multiple people at a time, but they should be designated for quiet. A garden or a fountain or a sculpture can be helpful, and that will differentiate this space from others, but it's not absolutely necessary. When people need quiet, the main thing that they need is quiet.

- **Design spaces that can flex from large group to small group on the fly.** That doesn't just mean flexibility to manage future changes in how people work or companies that add more employees. That means spaces that can flip from large group to small huddle within a minute. Effective collaboration often requires a converge/diverge process - everyone may start in a large group presentation, split into small groups to work on specific issues, reconvene to share findings and get feedback, etc. But far too many spaces accommodate the large group but work against the small group: large meeting rooms get noisy and people struggle to hear or be heard across the table (and imagine how impossible that would be if you had limited hearing or mobility to begin with). Being able to shift sound dampening, adjust task lighting for easier note-taking, and configure the space so that everyone in the small group can most effectively participate can make a great difference.

- **"Labs"** In conventional Innovation Districts, a Place that allows people to do some kind of specialized exploration often differentiates the "serious" innovation from more generic pursuits. A wet lab in a medical research center may make the latest technology available to its participants, but only a person with those special credentials (or well-placed friends) is going to be able to use them. If a non-medical innovator is pursuing an idea that requires a CAT scan, there's a good chance that person will drop the idea for lack of ability to access that tool, especially if that person does not look or sound like the acceptable people to use the lab.

Having a million dollar device in every Innovation District is not very practical, but a Future Ready Innovation District should provide easy access to the widest possible array of tools and "labs" it can. That's crucial to any innovator's ability to discover and test new ideas, but it's particularly important if we are serious about accelerating innovation. Consider how the following "labs" might help your Future Ready Innovation District tackle one of the emerging challenges we described in Part 1:

- A Makerspace with a woodshop, tools for carving foam into shapes, metal forming, laser cutting, 3D printing.
- A sewing lab
- A kitchen.
- A garden
- An art studio

How much easier would it be to test your prototype on a user if you could make a decent facsimile (not twine and Legos) right after you think of it? How much more effective would your efforts to ideate your new logo be if you had some good markers and large sheets of paper at hand, or you could pop onto a computer with the design suite that you can't afford yourself? What would you learn about a potential but unfamiliar market segment by making a favorite food with them?

Providing (and potentially staffing) these labs might be the most expensive part of the Future Ready Innovation District. I think they would be worth it for their ability to accelerate innovation. But as we noted before, given our lack of existing data, building these Labs flexible and small makes more sense than creating potential monuments to irrelevance.

- **Visitability.** If we are going to assert that the most effective innovation requires the broadest possible range of participants, then we have to make sure that our spaces throw up as few physical roadblocks to participation as possible.

  For a person in a motorized wheelchair, that step between the two old buildings that you combined to make your co working space may mean that they literally cannot enter half the building. For a person with auditory sensitivity, the level of echo in your hip post-industrial conference room may mean that all of your public events are off limits.

  Even if few of your full-time participants have mobility or sensory or cognitive differences, keep in mind that people will come to your buildings and participate in your events on an occasional basis, and that throwing up a barrier to even the casual visitor may mean that your participants lose an insight or an opportunity - an insight they will not find if they only interact with people who have the same abilities as they do. Widening the scope of the innovator logically requires a visitable building.

- **Physical Fitness**. One thing that we are learning about innovators and entrepreneurs is that many have relatively high levels of anxiety and depression, and that extended hours committed to building an innovation don't alleviate those conditions. We also know that physical exertion improves thinking and general cognition. Making it easy for innovators to stay physically active -whether through interesting and changing staircase walls or onsite tennis courts and weightlifting rooms - is likely to have nothing but benefits.

- **Porous**. A Future Ready Innovation District should present as few barriers to participation as possible. Public spaces should welcome anyone who wants to innovate, locks should appear on a few doors as possible, and event spaces should be easy for anyone inside or outside the District to attend. Multi-modal transportation systems can make a big difference in enabling a porous environment, making it easy both for participants to engage in the rest of the city, and for the rest of the city to discover their potential to innovate.

- **Careful of fads and trappings.** Designers and decision-makers who don't fully understand the intent of the Future Ready Innovation District may be tempted to trick it out in the trappings of people or places that they associate with "creatives." That might mean carefully-curated "urban" graffiti, oversized Chemex machines in the coffee shop, elaborate paver patterns on the sidewalk, or a host of other markers that will change as the definition of "cool" changes (as it always has).

Of course, there's nothing inherently wrong with hip hop-influenced murals, or methods for making coffee, or streetscape design. The challenge to watch out for, and to avoid like the plague, is the belief that such places will "make" an Innovation District a place where people want to come.

There's a tendency in urban and interior design to mistake a thing that sometimes shows up in a certain setting with a Sign that This is the Place Where Those Things Happen. Murals and coffee machines and the like do not create a Future Ready Innovation District, any more than donning a hat makes me a member of the English Peerage. But, in the throes of design, we can sometimes lose sight of the forest around our chosen trees.

- **Careful of Image Obsession**. Similarly, the inevitable pressure to build the Future Ready Innovation District's "Brand" can lead managers to pay a lot of attention to signage color schemes, logos and the number of social media hits. Again, there's nothing wrong (and a lot right) about a clear and distinctive visual palette, strong wayfinding, good logos and market outreach. But the common challenge is that designers and managers can mistake the outcomes for the impact, and doing that can both obscures the real impact or challenges and create a sense of a fake place, a false narrative.

- **Spaces that reinforce the culture and mission**. Many dedicated innovation spaces include photos of participants, motivational sayings, and other elements that try to convey the possibilities of the work going on. But these often just scratch the surface, especially if we are serious about not just doing any innovation, but doubling down on innovations that can have a significant impact on the community or the world.

What can we do with our spaces to continue to drive that sense of mission? To engage the members in exploring the horizons?

What about photos and stories of people who need innovations? Statistics and infographics? Places for participants to write their goals, visions, motivations, in a place where they will see what they wrote regularly?

We can become accustomed to unusual things pretty quickly, so just novelty isn't going to cut it, at least not in the long term. But temporary installations, even if they are no more than photos and paper, could be useful in jarring our thinking on a regular basis.

When

OK, we all know that most innovation doesn't happen on a 9 to 5 schedule. And many innovation Pumps (although not by any means all) seem to get that, and offer extended hours, a mix of daytime and evening events, etc. All well and good. But too often, program managers don't think about the following elements of their population:

- **People with children**. If you want people to be able to attend an evening event, perhaps child care would be helpful - especially if you are trying to attract more women, who still tend to carry the majority of child care duties in many households. Good and safe child care, however, isn't as simple as setting up some toys in a corner, so you may need to consider partnering with a person or organization with child care experience.

- **People who work second shift.** If all of your public events are in the evenings, you may be excluding a large number of potential innovators - from the assembly line worker tinkering on a new tool in her garage, to the ER doctor trying to design a new patient information system. Depending on the makeup of your local economy, an alternative schedule, or at least good archived video, may be helpful.

- **People who can't drive.** In many cities, public transportation options dwindle after 6:00 PM. Participants who don't drive or cannot drive may find it almost impossible to participate in events after conventional business hours.

- **People who are concerned about safety.** Not only women, but older and disabled participants may worry that they will be a crime target if they come to your evening event. That may not necessarily be an accurate perception - your urban location may suffer from an out-of-date stereotype or an unsavory history. But some attention to outdoor lighting, walkways to parking lots and bus stops, clear wayfinding signs and other ways to increase personal visibility and control may be very useful.

How

Now we get down to the hard part: paying for it.

If you look past the design finishes, the marketing campaigns, the food and beer and other high-visibility costs, you will find that most Innovation Districts spend their money on a relatively small set of features:

- Physical plant, including electric and internet,
- Staff, including program design and execution,
- Materials, including coffee and lab equipment,
- Event costs, including speaker honoraria and drinks.

And that's about it. Pretty simple, really. A Future-Ready Innovation District probably invests somewhat more in staff and materials, given the What and Where priorities we've identified, but the basic distribution will be about the same.

The problem is that at least some of the innovators who are looking for support are, almost by their nature, in need of something that they can't provide by themselves. And as we discussed before, since network benefits are poorly accounted for in our Industrial Era bookkeeping, innovation districts often tend to be funded by grants or corporate sponsorship. They rely on funding given to them by another entity - a big business, a foundation, a government agency.

That gives them a fundamental problem: *They are not viewed as being central to the future of the larger community, and thus they are often expected to get by with funding at the minimal level possible.*

That's not a judgement; it's a factor of that basic economic structure clash we talked about in Part 1. But to make sure we understand how we got in this situation, let's review that underlying clash again, this time in the light of how it will affect your Future Ready Innovation District if you don't actively work against it.

It's such a base assumption, it sounds almost banal to write it out:

Economically, we place the central value on one specific type of exchange: the buyer-seller relationship. Supply and demand.

Under our economic structures, built on the fundamentals of Adam Smith-style economics, anything that falls outside of buying something from someone else, or selling something to someone else, is an "externality." It falls outside of the central transaction. It might be nice, it might even be morally right or politically necessary, but it has little or no "real" value.

And if it's not considered valuable, it's not something worth putting more than token money into.

This is a key element of why charitable or social good activities are so badly underfunded - - They're assumed to be pleasant or nice, but not generating meaningful value.

This basic assumption creates a grossly outmoded, oversimplistic and externality-accelerating set of assumptions. It creates as a logical outcome a devaluing of any activities that aren't directly tied to a customer-seller transaction. This assumption conveniently overlooked a lot of pretty nasty externalities in the Industrial Era (look up child mortality for a New England state in the 1880s or read a report on a Superfund site) But it's an even worse idea in the Fusions Era for many reasons - including one that's very, very practical:

Almost no business today can control their entire production process, a la Carnegie or Ford. Every business, largest to smallest, is inextricably wound into the ecosystem. Even an Amazon or a Google depends on the participation of thousands of independent operators - - not just buyers, as in the Industrial Era, but as *co-creators of the product.* If independent suppliers stopped selling on Amazon, or if web content creators stopped embedding Google Maps, those companies would have only a fraction of the value that they enjoy today. Amazon and Google derive their value from their ability to be a *platform* for others value generators. Rockefeller's Standard Oil did not make it easier for small well owners to make money off their crude - - more often, they ran the small competitors out of business. Standard Oil was an industrial era business icon. It was definitely not a platform.

The plus side of depending on an ecosystem of suppliers and service providers is that you don't have to maintain the whole thing yourself. The downside is that you take a hit every time the ecosystem gets hurt. We haven't fully internalized that learning yet, but we see it in action every time a tariff leads to layoffs, or a factory closing kills off a dozen small parts suppliers, or a couple of decades of poor schooling results in businesses unable to find innovation-ready employees. We have a dependency on the health of the ecosystem

As a result of our failure to recognize that we are not independent operators, but instead dependents of the ecosystem, we under-value the systems that we need the most, now and increasingly in the future. We end up funding the crucial infrastructure of the next economic era - the infrastructure that should be enabling a new explosion of the innovation we desperately need - by scraping for spare change.

If that weren't enough of a mismatch, we should also remember that nonprofit-style funding is inherently unstable, especially in a world where the deferred maintenance of social services, education, tax systems, etc. are becoming impossible to ignore. Public grants get cut on a regular basis. Charities and foundations shift their focus to some new, more crisis-y issue. And as we discussed previously, making an airtight demonstration of our innovation infrastructure's impact has not often been anyone's real priority.

That's a lot of high level preamble, but I did that recap to demonstrate that we have to shift our thinking to a funding model that fits this moment in time, not an inconsistent, leftover model that claims to value innovation but has not yet learned to connect its claims with its actions. That goes for our funders and our partners, but it also goes for us.

In 75 years, perhaps our economic models will have caught up and our systems for paying for innovation infrastructure will jive with our claims, but in the intervening time, we're going to have to learn to play by a mix of the new and the old sets of assumptions. And that means that we have to

- Demonstrate unmistakeable value of our work.
- Change the framing of what that unmistakable value means to connect the emerging understanding of ecosystem dependence to actual value.

In the interim, it's going to be a little awkward, but we can't allow ourselves to continue to be defined as externalities, as nice-to-haves. That way lies irrelevance.

The right funding and support mix will depend on the community, its history and its relationships. But here are some elements that will help:

- **Maintain a portfolio of funding sources**. Organizations of many types get into trouble when they depend on one or two income sources. More funding streams may mean more complicated bookkeeping and more time spent on reporting and relationship-maintaining, but it also maintains your ability to pivot if needed - and to bounce back if a funding source dries up.

- **Design the work that your piece of the infrastructure does so that it is not just about running programs, but so that you are providing a real, definable, measurable value directly to potential funders (especially for-profit funders).** That may take some work - and you might end up with a program that doesn't look like ones you encounter at conferences. But there should be some value that you can provide, especially given the emergence of an ecosystem-driven economy.

What suppliers are your larger businesses struggling to find? How do they find help leveraging new technologies? Are businesses struggling to find good employees, and if so how can you help ease that friction? If you start from an understanding of what your funders need help with to make a successful Fusion Economy transition, you will be able to find ways to leverage your network and relationships to help them -- and you will be able to attach a reasonable value to that help, both for other ecosystem members and for yourself.

- **Help your businesses address their increasing pressure to center inclusion and diversity.** Whether it's a tech start-up, a marketing agency or a mainline manufacturer, businesses are facing pressure- from their investors, their employees, their market research and more - to connect to people from diverse backgrounds. And, given that business leadership is still disproportionately white and male, they will probably value help. If your participants are as fully diverse as they should be, and if you have demonstrated that yours is a place where diverse innovators can find a home, then your organization can play a vital role in helping organizations whose leadership is not diverse learn to understand and provide solutions to people whom they might never have encountered otherwise.

This work needs to be done within a culture and in a manner that values diverse contributions, especially from people who have been historically overlooked or disadvantaged, and it's crucial that your organization makes sure that they are treated with honor, value and with respect as innovators who have unique and valuable insight. But don't forget: this isn't charity or do-gooding - these connections are of real value to the Fusion Era businesses who need them, and that value should not be discounted. For them, for you, and for the diverse innovators with new insight. Think back to the Think Tank model we discussed in a previous chapter - that shifts the power and the value in a way that honestly benefits everyone.

- **Charge fair prices for services.** In the 1990s and 2000s, entrepreneurship organizations often set up incubators - typically space for new businesses offered at very cheap prices for as long as the business wanted. But not only did these early incubators often fail to make enough income to be self-sufficient, they also telegraphed an unintended message to both tenants and funders: *We aren't developing sustainable businesses. We are doing charity.* That meant that many business tenants saw no incentive to move out, and funding usually remained at barely the amount needed to keep the lights on, at best.

  Pumps today tend to avoid the old incubator errors, but we often find that many Pumps, especially those that have nonprofit funding, continue to operate on a charity mindset. Fees for services across the board tend to be lower than market rate - sometimes through subsidy, but often at least in part through operating on a minimal basis[27]. In reality, some participants could probably pay a good deal more, and doing so would not only help the bottom line, but it would help change the messaging - from

---

[27] I referenced Vu Le's *Nonprofit AF* blog previously. If you want to see a great demonstration of the pernicious impact of this charity mindset, look up his articles on office chairs. Seriously.

threadbare begging to an organization that provides a definite value.

Having said that, though, it's clear that increasing access for historically disadvantaged and excluded populations means embracing the participation of people who aren't able to pay close to full freight. In a Fusion Era mindset, however, subsidizing their involvement is not charity, it's a good business investment, because we need their insight and participation. As I've now noted several times, enabling a business to meaningfully connect to diverse populations is increasingly, directly tied to increased access to funding and markets, and increased ability to create valuable products and services. So that's not charity, that's an advantage.

- **Be very careful in accepting nonprofit and government grants or funding.** This sounds like a contradiction to what I just said, and some of you who have spent your careers in nonprofit or government might find this unnerving. But hear me out.

I have spent most of my career working with governments and nonprofits. Both kinds of organizations do important work that we desperately need - and in a Fusion Era, ecosystem-dependent world saddled with the unaddressed externalities of the Industrial Era, we need the services and the support that nonprofits and governments provide more than ever. And I adamantly believe that our efforts in coming years to help them to work in a Fusion Era-appropriate manner will be worth everything we put into it.

But at the moment, the majority of government programs and nonprofit or philanthropic funds are stuck in an Industrial Era model. That is not to say that they are not trying to solve important challenges and foster innovative solutions - many are. But it is to say that the methods that they are using, and the systems that they are using to administer and evaluate their work, are mismatched to the manner in which we need to operate.

Take a typical grant application for example -- let's say, for an entrepreneurship training Program. Whether it's a government fund or a foundation, the process is going to look largely like this:

- Complete exhaustive application that outlines a proposed Program in detail, specifies deliverables and outputs and very concrete measures, and includes extensive documentation of community support, socioeconomic data, history of successfully administered grants, etc.

- Negotiate with funder to adjust time lines, outputs, rhetoric, etc. to more closely align with a predetermined set of priorities or types of work that the administrative regulations say can be funded (and if it's a competitive grant, all of the work to this point may be for nothing if grant goes to someone else)

- Conduct the Program as closely as possible to what the funder approved.

- Complete extensive reporting to the funder that attempts to prove that what you said you would deliver is exactly what you have done. While bearing in mind that the funder has probably not encountered your Program in person, or talked to you in months.

People who have worked in nonprofits can explain to you exactly how the grant funding strategy saps staff's time and energy away from the work they are supposed to be doing. But for Innovation Infrastructure leadership, there's an even deeper problem.

The process that I outlined above *assumes predictability* -- it is based on the expectation that you will be able to execute precisely according to plan. If you do not execute according to plan, you will spend extra time in the reporting explaining (or spinning) what happened, in the hopes that the funder does not cut you out in the future.

We've already said that building the Innovation Infrastructure that we need - and accelerating into the Fusion Economy as fast as we need to - means that we have to give up our assumptions of predictability and learn to work in a resilient manner. We know this so well that we coach our businesses to use Lean Startup-type methods -- make little bets, pilot, evaluate, pivot, etc.

But our nonprofit Innovation Infrastructure elements often keep doing the same programs, the same suite of events, season after season. Why do we not do as we have told others to do?

The answer often lies in that nonprofit or government funding process. If you're going to have to report why you changed your tactics, justify the fact that you didn't do the things they funded you to do, risk the funder's criticism or rejection, then perhaps we should just keep doing what we were doing - maybe tweak it a little, somewhere they won't notice, so that we don't get cut off. And if you're going to have to spring that unpleasant news on them after radio silence for the last several months, it's even less appealing to make the kinds of course corrections that we often know in our guts that we need to do.

An effective funder- fundee relationship in a Fusion Era environment has to look different from what we've learned to expect. An effective funder - one who is truly advancing our movement into the Fusion Economy

- **Will stay close.** They won't rely on a yearly reporting process built around the assumption that nothing will change between award and program close. They'll know what's going on at least from one month to the next.

- **Will engage actively.** They won't just write a check and go back to the office. They'll directly observe, they'll participate, they'll provide a valuable outside perspective and connect the fundee with their network of other philanthropists, foundations, agencies.

- **Will truly value and embrace transparency**, especially when things are not going as planned. Instead of saying they want transparency and then penalizing the fundee when reality diverges from expectation, an effective funder will jump into the opportunity to learn from the experience.

- **Will be able to pivot with you.** Instead of struggling with its internal accountability systems, an effective funder will be able to shift directions with you mid-grant.

- **Will challenge itself.** A funder in the Fusion Era will have to maintain the same openness, lack of hubris and ability to get outside of its own unexamined assumptions as every other entity, if it is going to be an accelerator of innovation and not a drag on forward momentum. An effective funder is going to have to be able to shift, sometimes very profoundly, when it learns that its original assumptions were wrong.

I don't doubt that many individual grant administrators and program directors will see the necessity of these points - many already do, and they're trying to meet these needs. But they're often doing so from within an ironclad box of reporting requirements, Board directives, accounting protocols, and more. Far too often, government and nonprofit innovators are pushing against the most rigid constraints facing anyone working on the next economy.

That's why I said that enabling these sectors will be so crucial to our long-term success - especially as we are addressing the massive and pervasive externalities that the Industrial Era has left us. If it sounds a little like venture capital to you, there's a reason for that - the VC process, for all its limitations, was built around an ecosystem-based, network-dependent set of assumptions. But for government and nonprofits to make this kind of transition *without losing sight of their larger public purpose,* that's going to be very hard work- in terms of organizations, possibly the hardest work facing us in the Fusion Era.

So that's also why I advised you not to rely on them if you can at all help it. As we often tell our entrepreneurs, it won't help you to try to boil the ocean.

So what should our funding look like? Broadly, I think it's important to make sure that our Future Ready Innovation District, and all of our Pumps, build toward three broad channels of support :

- Partners to whom we are providing economically significant value
- Sponsorships of events that are energizing the whole community - everyone, not just our inner circle - about our shared future
- Targeted support for people who have been left out of innovation in the past - not just because it's nice, but because we need the value that they, uniquely, can add to the equation.

Too many Pumps struggle and fail to achieve what we need them to do - not because they can't support themselves, but because , just like we talked about in Part 1, they unthinkingly defaulted to an Industrial Era model to underpin Fusion Era growth. We try to put a steam engine in a jet aircraft, and when the contraption doesn't work the way it should, we spend our time trying to tweak the fittings and adjust the fuel mixture, instead of figuring out how to get to our destination with something that actually fits the vehicle.

Sometimes we stick with the steam engine because we know how steam engines work - even if they're not working in this context. There's a certain comfort, a confidence in knowing how to work the dials and the valves. But if the steam engine is the wrong power source, we are not doing ourselves or anyone else any favors.

Why

If you've stuck with me this long, I suspect you've got the Why.

You understand that our economy and culture and communication and technology are already changing, that they're changing in ways that we don't always understand or manage well, and that all of these basic building blocks of our lives seem to be on a track to be fundamentally different in 5, 10, 50 years.

And you understand that the stakes of failing to understand this sea change, of hanging on to old assumptions that clash with the emerging, of taking a lackadaisical approach and letting the chips fall where they may... that none of these will be good for us. For any of us.

You understand that we have made some decent early efforts to build the Innovation Infrastructure that we need going into this new era, and you have a fairly clear-eyed view of their strengths and shortcomings. And you know at least somewhat how we can work on making it better.

So now all that remains is to accelerate.

Epilogue

When you write a book, there are moments when you wish you could jump out of the pages, crouch down across the table from the reader, and implore them

"Do you get it??? Do you understand??? Did that make sense???"

Because you never truly know if you do. That's part of the challenge of using an Industrial Age method for sharing information in an emerging world that expects direct, intimate, immediate communication. This is why writers develop a lot of neuroses.

Hopefully, this made sense. Hopefully it will also make more sense in five, 10, 20 years, as some of these issues unfold more fully. Maybe I'll have turned out to get a whole lot of things wrong. I have a book on my shelf from the 1930s that sings the praises of the French Maginot Line, a huge fortification system that was supposed to prevent the Germans from ever invading again. The Germans just went around it. Trying to write about the future is its own kind of long-term humiliation.

But here's the important part: I believe in you. I believe that you, all of you who care about a healthy and resilient future, about your communities and your entrepreneurs and your creators, have an incredible and usually overlooked reservoir of innovation yourselves. In my career, I've watched thousands of committed people change places, change people, change communities. And far too often, doing all that within structures and systems and assumptions about how the world works that tie one of their hands behind their back. I know that much, much more is possible than senior staff and leadership and officials and Big Deals insist is possible. I didn't just believe that; people a lot like you showed it to me.

And the Fusion Era looks like it will work in your favor. As we all become mass communicators, as we learn to lean into the power of networks, as we unlock the power of transparency and learn to leverage every person's innovative potential, much of what we are scrapping to get done today should become, in at least some respects, easier. That can be hard to see right now, when we are in this messy, often violently chaotic moment where the old system's beneficiaries are lashing out and the new system's advocates are still finding their voice.

But as we've explored in this book, it's happening, and it will happen. We don't exactly know what it will look like, but it's becoming clearer every day.

I don't worry so much about old power players clinging to what they have. I don't worry, in the part of my head that's focused on our future, so much about the clashes and squabbles that often seem to define the moment.

You don't have to be a history professor to know that those tempests are going to be footnotes before long.

What I do think about, when I think about our transition to the Fusion Age, is this: despite our best intentions, we have the potential to be our own worst enemy. We are wired by our evolution to seek patterns, to slide into repeat actions, to use our ability to make sense of the world around us to set up rules of thumb and follow then on auto-pilot. We like to stick to the familiar. We like to sleep walk whenever we can. This is part of why our Innovation infrastructure has often fallen short of what we needed: we use old systems, like the funding issues in the last chapter, without critically examining whether they actually fit the new situation.

Not sleepwalking, not working reflexively from our assumptions, is hard. Really hard. Exhaustingly hard. But that's exactly what we have to do

Previous era transitions took hundreds of years, to a great extent because people like to sleepwalk. It took generations to change our basic assumptions and work out the discrepancies between what we were saying and how we were doing it. The kinds of discrepancies that I've been describing all through this book.

But as we reviewed in Part 1, we don't have the luxury of that much time this time. We have very significant global challenges that won't wait a couple hundred years for us to get our heads around the necessity of solving them. We have to accelerate innovation, because the externalities of the Industrial Era constitute very real threats to all of us.

Our greatest source of that acceleration isn't going to be in think tanks or universities or government programs or big businesses. It will be in unlocking all of us, regardless of our background or education or priviledge or lack thereof, to work our network, command our communication and information, and learn from minds that are as different from our own as we can find.

Our greatest source is going to be you.

That's how we accelerate innovation.

Let's go get 'em.

-dgr

Here's what people who are working on the ground
in real communities today have to say about
Everybody Innovates Here:

Everybody Innovates Here rightfully questions common assumptions about how innovation occurs. It provides an extremely helpful road map to making more effective use of our most precious resources: People.

Mark Barbash, FM, Director of the Ohio Economic Development Institute at Ohio Economic Development Association

This book is a fresh approach to innovation. Della challenges us to think about the infrastructure of innovation and our assumptions through a new and more interconnected framework that grows resilience.

Jennifer Kime, Downtown Mansfield, Inc.

"Innovation" is one of the most talked-about concepts, but the least understood. Della Rucker guides readers through what it takes to place innovation at the center of building strong, resilient local economies. This is must reading for anyone hoping to participate and compete in a new economy where innovation matters.

Isaac Kremer, Downtown Metuchen

Wise Fool
Press

173

www.ingramcontent.com/pod-product-compliance
Lightning Source LLC
Chambersburg PA
CBHW072033190526
45165CB00017B/524